GHOSTS OF THE RIALTO

To
MARGOT
(Contessa de Asarta Guiccioli)

'L'ombra sua torna, ch'era dipartita'
DANTE
Inferno—Canto IV.81

'The soul's Rialto hath its merchandise'
E. B. BROWNING
Sonnets from the Portuguese

CONTENTS

CONTENTS

ILLUSTRATIONS

PREFACE

'Do you believe in ghosts?' asked Mr. Mulliner abruptly.

I weighed the question carefully. I was a little surprised, for nothing in our previous conversation had suggested the topic.

'Well,' I replied. 'I don't like them, if that's what you mean. I was once butted by one, as a child.'

'Ghosts. Not goats.'

'Oh, ghosts? Do I believe in ghosts?'

'Exactly.'

'Well, yes-and-no.'

P. G. WODEHOUSE—'Honeysuckle Cottage'
(in *Meet Mr. Mulliner*)

THIS book of mine is the second I have written about ghosts. If I were asked if I believed in them, I would have to say: 'Yes', for once I saw one and heard it speak. This little private ghost-story of mine might serve as an opening to *Ghosts of the Rialto*, even though it takes one far away from Venice. But two of the people mentioned in the following pages—the Marchese Alessandro Guiccioli and his wife Olga—were my hosts in the Italian Embassy at Tokyo, shortly before the outbreak of the First World War.

The First Interpreter, Gasco, asked me out to dinner, explaining that we could not dine at his own house in the Embassy grounds, because his cook was ill, indeed very ill, and his old mother had been called in to look after him.

So Gasco and I went off in a car. He took me first to see the tombs of the Forty-seven Ronin, and then to dine at Omori, in a restaurant overlooking the bay. It was dark when we got home, but not quite dark, for the month was June, when nights are short. Having put his car in the Embassy garage, Gasco took me round to his own quarters for a chat and a drink.

We approached his house from the back, and as we did so, I heard him give a sudden exclamation of annoyance.

'What's the matter?' I asked.

'It's Micheda, my cook. He ought to be in bed, and there he is, leaning out of the window in the night air.'

'Well, it's warm enough anyway.'

'But it's silly of him. What's the good of his mother coming here to look after him, if she lets him do things like that!'

Gasco walked up to the side of the house and spoke to the cook at the window. There was no light in the room behind him, and the garden paths, such as the one we were walking on, were lighted only in front of the various buildings. But we could see Micheda's head and shoulders quite plainly, for he was wearing what appeared to be a white kimono, and round his head was a white cloth (or handkerchief), with two little pointed ends, sticking up like ears.

Gasco said something to him in Japanese, which I could not understand, for I knew only a few words of the language, such as a tourist picks up here and there: the ordinary forms of salutation and the names of the more common necessities of domestic life.

Micheda did not answer, but as we turned away, he said quite clearly:

'*Sayonara!*' ('Goodbye')

Gasco preceded me into the house, and when we reached the sitting room, he gave orders that the sick man's mother should be sent to him. She came, a frail little old woman, looking tired and unhappy, yet wearing on her face the usual ceremonial smile that serves the Japanese as a mask, under all circumstances.

Again I did not understand a word of what Gasco said to her, nor of her brief answer, but something in the utter astonishment and horror in his face gave me a first inkling of the truth.

Micheda had died three hours before, shortly after we had left the house.   D. V.

Rome

February 1956

I

THE ARGONAUTS

Wie werd'ich je die grosse Rätsel fassen?
AUGUST VON PLATEN,
on arriving in Venice

VENICE is a riddle with many solutions. Each of us finds his own.

One afternoon, I had been to the railway-station to see somebody off, and had come out again on the side of the Grand Canal. It was my intention to make my way home on foot, through the narrow *calli* that branch off behind the church of San Simeone Piccolo. But my attention was caught by the sight of two young men, who evidently had just arrived. They were carrying some shapeless bales, wrapped in tarpaulin, which they deposited near the steps that lead down to the water, and then proceeded to unpack.

From their fair hair and general appearance, I guessed they must be Germans, and their subsequent actions were characteristic of the initiative and the *laboriositas* that Leibniz describes as a virtue of the Teutonic races.

They had come to Venice from their native land, bringing a boat, in which to row about the city where the streets are the sea. The boat, or canoe, was in three pieces that had to be screwed together. How this could be done efficiently, to prevent the vessel leaking, I cannot think. But in due course, the navigators launched their craft, got into it with their belongings and started gaily up the Grand Canal in the direction of the Rialto.

While they were carrying it down to the water, I happened to notice that their boat had a name painted on the bows. It was called *Argo*. Its young owners must have been poets, to compare themselves to the heroes who sailed with Jason, to seek the Golden Fleece.

I believe that later they had some trouble with the police. To navigate that labyrinth of waterways, a boat must have a licence, like a motor-car on land. But in the end those Argonauts were authorized to carry out their plan, and visit Venice, paddling their own canoe.

What, if anything, did they know of the town they were approaching? I hope they did not know much. I would like to think that, as the shadows lengthened, they met the ghosts of the Rialto and heard each of them tell their story. Thus would they drink deep from the Pierian spring, the fountain-head of knowledge, pure and undefiled!

The *Argo* disappeared round the bend, opposite the *campo* of San Marcuola (a composite abbreviation for the names of two saints, Ermegora and Fortunato). There one might meet the characters out of a real ghost-story. It tells how the parish-priest was dragged out of bed and kicked and cuffed by the corpses buried in his church, for having said, in a sermon: 'Where the dead are, they stay!': a statement no self-respecting spectre could tolerate.

Our Argonauts would hardly take interest in such old-wives' tales. They would seek the ghosts of countrymen of their own: Goethe, Nietsche, Richard Wagner, or—to go further back—Albrecht Dürer, whose copper-plate engraving, *The Knight and Death*, had for its inspiration the equestrian statues of Francesco Sforza (now lost) and of Bartolommeo Colleoni.

On their reaching Rialto, there would be light enough still for the Argonauts to admire the Annunciation sculptured on the bridge: the Angel at one end, the Virgin at the other and the dove hovering over the centre of the span. The *Argo* would be moored to an iron ring near the steps that lead up to the Riva del Vin, and its navigators would go ashore, to meet, not our present-day Venetians, but ladies wearing Longhi masks, each accompanied by her *cavalier servente*. They might notice three tall bearded figures, men with faces browned by Eastern suns: the first white men ever to see the Pacific Ocean. Their surname was Polo, and they had just come home after an absence of twenty-four years, bringing a collection of travellers' tales that their fellow-citizens had some difficulty in swallowing. They talked of a black stone that could be dug out of the earth and burnt for fires, and spoke of fountains in the Caucasus that spouted oil instead of water.

They are rather confusing, these ghosts of the Rialto, for they belong to every century since the year 840 after the birth of Christ, down to present-day. It follows that they must be a mixed lot, in an extraordinary variety of costumes. If the Argonauts came from Dresden, they might recognize Caterina Cornaro, bejewelled Queen of Cyprus, as she steps out of her gondola. The picture gallery in their native town has a portrait of her by Titian.

Near the sculptured figure of the hunchback (who, by the way, is not a hunchback at all), called *Il Gobbo del Rialto*, an English peer is taking notes for a book of travel, in verse, to be called *Childe Harold's Pilgrimage*.

Close by, in the Campo San Bartolommeo, two Venetians of the nineteenth century—say in 1847—are escorting an English visitor, by name Richard Cobden. He is being much fêted in Venice, and a banquet has been organized for him, on the Giudecca; each of the assembled guests has to wear an ear of corn in his button-hole, as a reminder that this great liberal had succeeded in passing some 'corn laws', for the benefit of his countrymen. The Venetians acting as his hosts are Daniele Manin and Giambattista Varè. They also are liberals, and suspected by the Austrian police of wishing to start a revolution to restore their country's independence.

Besides historical figures, our young Argonauts might meet the ghosts of fiction (they are quite as real as the others): Jessica, spending Shylock's ducats in the shops of the Rialto; Othello, just betrothed to Desdemona, striding proudly through the crowd, with Jago at his heels. *La Locandiera*, most attractive of boardinghouse landladies, who lets out rooms to unattached gentlemen. Goldoni made her live for us, and Eleonora Duse acted the part, which was one of her favourites.

Venice has, naturally, old ghost-stories of her own, which everyone on Rialto knows, and her saints are much to the fore in them. One of these inspired Giorgione to paint a picture, now in the Accademia. It is called 'St. Mark and the Fisherman'. This is the story:

On the 25th February 1340 there was a terrible storm over the lagoons, and in Venice the waters rose higher than ever in the memory of man. An old fisherman had fastened his boat to the Riva di San Marco and there awaited the passing of the storm. Then there came to him an unknown man, who asked him to row him over to San Giorgio Maggiore, saying that it was the will of God and that he would be well paid. Though in great fear, the fisherman consented. When his customer landed, he left him and returned with another, younger man. And he said: 'Now row towards San Niccolò di Lido.' But the fisherman answered: 'How can one possibly go so far, with one oar?' But they reassured him, saying: 'Row boldly, for it is possible, and you shall be well paid.' And they started off, and though the storm still raged, the waters all around them were smooth.

At San Niccolò di Lido, the two passengers picked up a third and commanded the fisherman to row out to the open sea, between the two castles, that defend the entrance to the lagoons. And still the tempest continued with unabated fury. A strange bark was approaching: an enormous galleon, loaded with demons, making their way to Venice, to destroy it utterly. But the three men whom the fisherman was rowing

6

made the sign of the cross and exorcised the demons, so that the galleon vanished. Then the three commanded the fisherman to land them, each where he had embarked. When he had done so, the fisherman asked to be paid. The first man he had taken on board said to him: 'I am St. Mark, the protector of this City; the other is the brave knight St. George, and he whom we left on the Lido, is St. Nicholas, the patron saint of sailors. Say to the Doge and to the Procuratore that they are to pay you, and say likewise that this tempest arose because of a certain schoolmaster, dwelling at San Felice, who sold his soul to the devil, and afterwards hanged himself.'

The fisherman demurred, saying: 'If I tell them, they will not believe.'

Then St. Mark took a ring off his finger and said: 'Show them this, and tell them when they look in the Sacristy where the treasure is kept, they will not find it.' Thereupon he disappeared.

Next day, the fisherman presented himself to the Doge and related all he had seen, showing the ring for a sign. And the Treasurer, having sought for the ring in the usual place, found it not. Then the fisherman was paid and a life-provision made for him in his old age. And a solemn procession was ordained, to give thanks to God.

*   *   *

Another ghost story explains the name given to one of the *valli* or deep canals that intersect the lagoons and make them navigable even to big ships. It was told to Horatio Brown (author of *Life on the Lagoons*) by his gondolier, Antonio Salin.

Six men were out fishing, and they had a little boy to cook for them, so as to have breakfast ready in a tiny hut, when they returned there before dawn. One night, these fishermen, having taken up their nets, were rowing back to their hut, when they saw a dead man floating on the water. They dragged the corpse into the boat, where it lay in the prow, the head resting on the arms. The boy had a meal waiting, but when the six men sat down to it, he asked where their companion was, for he had seen seven in the boat. The fishermen played a grim joke on him, saying:

'Go down and call him, saying breakfast is ready.'

The boy went down to the shore and called, but of course there was no answer. He came back and said so. The fishermen sent him down again, telling him to shout louder and to ask if they had to wait till doomsday for him. This time the boy came back and said: 'It is all right, he is coming up now.'

The men turned pale and looked at one another without speaking. And soon they heard footsteps on the path. The door was pushed open, and the dead man came and sat down at table, in the seventh place, which was the one that the boy had left vacant. The others gazed at him without being able to move, or speak. The blood ran cold in their veins, and before the sun had risen high in the heavens, there were seven dead men round the table.

Ever since, the *valle* where stood the little hut has been called *La Valle dei Sette Morti*: the Valley of the Seven Dead Men.

The lonely expanse and eerie desolation, described in this story, are in startling contrast with all the gilded splendour that we naturally associate with Venice.

2

GHOST OF THE *SERENISSIMA*

Of all the ghosts of the Rialto, the first is Venice herself. For Venice died on the 17th October 1797, when she ceased to be a sovereign power and became only a town: a strange and beautiful town, whose structures rise out of the sea, as a coral island does, built by marine organisms. The palaces are still there, the canals, the Piazza, the *campi* and *campielli* and the re-built Campanile. Their wonder leaps upon the foreigner as he comes out of the station, or parks his car—if he can find room—at the end of, or on, the bridge to the mainland.

Think what the impression on the traveller must have been, before that bridge was built! An uncle of my father's was responsible for the innovation, but even so, I cannot but regret the days when one took a gondola from Mestre, or a boat from Fusina. A vast sheet of water stretched away to the horizon, bordered only by a chain of low-lying, almost invisible islets in the east. The sea, calm and shimmering, with countless ripples, mirrored the sky above and took on the lights of dawn and sunset. Masses of seaweed rose and fell, with the incoming or outgoing tides, like some dark animal breathing (there is a church on a lonely islet, called 'Our Lady of the Seaweed'). A distant background of encircling Alps—the snow-covered peaks of the Cadore—melted into the clouds to the west.

Other towns stand on the edge of the water and are built along canals that penetrate inland. The green and gold spires of Copenhagen, the palaces of Stockholm, even the curved roofs and the pagodas of Swatow, are mirrored in the water.

But they were born on land. Only Venice rose from the sea itself, foam-born, like Aphrodite.

It is not surprising that literary people should feel inspired to write her history, nor that they should so rarely succeed.

The old histories of Venice are mostly very long and very dull. Nobody knows this better than myself, for I inherited from my Venetian ancestors a vast library of annals and chronicles, bound in brown leather and tarnished gold. Whenever I open a page, here and there, I seem to find nothing but accounts of battles.

Though continually at war with some other power, the Venetian Republic was known as *la Serenissima*, 'the most Serene'; a qualification which implies an unruffled and tranquil state of mind and an enviable security. Yet at the time when the Venetian chronicles were compiled, people assumed that any revision of existing political situations could only be effected by wars. Nowadays, we create international institutions to accomplish the purpose peacefully. But the prospect is much the same, even though recent world-wars have shown us that, in the present state of the world, nobody can win.

I regret to say that—as far as I am concerned—most of the volumes of my old library belong to the 'great unread'. My ancestors had more leisure than I have. Life is now too hurried to struggle with works in twelve, twenty-five, and even more, large tomes. And the vellum-bound French Encyclopaedias that preceded (and, to a certain extent, contributed to) the French Revolution, are too much out of date to be worth consulting except by bibliomaniacs and students of social history. Despite his delight in browsing among the stands of the *bouquinistes*, on the embankment of the Seine, I doubt if even that fictitious character, the Abbé Coignard, would have had the patience to settle down with these volumes. As imagined by Anatole France, the Abbé had no illusions concerning the lessons that history can teach. And he once told his disciple, Jacques Tournebroche, the following story:

The young prince Zémire, having succeeded his father on the throne of Persia, sent for the wisest Academicians of the empire, and said to them:

'I have been taught by my good tutor, Doctor Zèb, that the monarchs of the world would be less exposed to the danger of errors of judgment, if they were enlightened by the example of the Past. Go therefore and prepare for me a Universal History, and make sure that you omit nothing that should ensure its being complete.'

The wise men promised to do all that was in their power to please the prince, and they retired to accomplish the task he had set them.

After twenty years, they came back with a string of twelve camels, each laden with 500 fat volumes. Besides these, there was one camel who could barely carry the Preface to the *magnum opus*, and another camel groaning under the burden of the Index.

The Permanent Secretary of the Academy prostrated himself humbly on the steps of the Throne, and assured his master that in those volumes was contained all that was known about the customs of peoples and the vicissitudes of Empires. But the Shah stared at the camels pessimistically. And though he thanked the Academicians for collecting all that valuable material, he professed himself too busy with affairs of State to be able to read so much prose.

'While you laboured,' he said, 'I have been growing old and am now half way through life. These books shall be stored in the Imperial Archives. Please prepare me an abridgment, more in keeping with the brevity of our existence here below.'

So the wise Academicians set to work once more, and after another twenty years they turned up again with 1,500 volumes, piled on the humps of three camels. 'Sire!', said the Permanent Secretary, in a voice that lacked the strength and the assurance of former days, 'here is an abridged edition of your History. Again we feel sure that nothing essential has been omitted.'

'That may be,' said the Shah. 'But again it is too long for me to read. Cut it short, if you wish me to learn, ere I die, the history of mankind.'

This time the Permanent Secretary appeared after five years, walking painfully with the aid of crutches, and leading a small donkey with one fat volume on its back.

As he entered the palace, a chamberlain said to him: 'Hurry, for the Shah is dying!'

And indeed, the Shah lay on his death-bed. With half-blind eyes, he gazed on the book that had been brought to him. And he groaned.

'I must die without knowing the history of men!'

The Permanent Secretary, who was nearing his end no less than his Sovereign-Lord, answered: 'Sire, I can sum up, in a few words, all the books can teach us. *Men are born, and they suffer, and they die!*' And thus, late in life, the Shah learnt all there is in Universal History.

It is with some such amiable scepticism that I regard my old Venetian library, even if I feel that somewhere on those dusty shelves, there lurks the ghost of *la Serenissima*. Now and then, as the weather darkens, I open a page here and there.

C. Sallustii Crispi—Coniuratio Catilinae et Bellum Jugurthinum— This is an Aldine, printed in Venice in 1538. Someone has scrawled his name—quite illegibly—across the anchor and porpoise that were the printer's trade-mark. Then comes a Euclid, one of the first to be printed, bound in red leather, with a coat-of-arms engraved in gold. Here are four volumes, with coloured maps and towns and little figures of the citizens standing in the foreground. Volume I begins with London: *Londinium, feracissimi Angliae Regni Metropolis.* Only one bridge spans the Thames, and that looks as if it were laid on boats. On the 'South Warke' side of the river, there are very few houses, and plenty of green fields. The 'Towre' looks imposing, but the town itself is very small, surrounded by a wall with gates in it. Near the river-bank is the chapel belonging to the House of Savoy.

Half-way through this volume are Dresden and Leipzig, the former hardly as long as the Elbe is broad. It is when we get to the East that the towns are depicted in minute detail and with greatest realism: Constantinople, Aden, Mombaza. . . . In the plan of Jerusalem there is an inset representing Moses obtaining the Tables of the Covenant on Mount Sinai; also a High Priest of Israel in his ceremonial robes.

Even the towns of the newly discovered continent of America are there: *Cuzco—Regni Peru in Novo Orbe Caput; Mexico—Regia et Celebris Hispaniae novae Civitatis.* . . .

Such pictures combine to form a time-machine, ready to take one for long-distance rides, to meet the ghosts of the Past. The years and the generations fold themselves up like a telescope. In another sense, it is so in my own family. My father was sixty-seven when he died, having been born in September 1817. His life and mine cover already 140 years. This is a far longer period than the average covered by two successive generations. If you add my grandfather and his elder brother, we go back to the time when, in Venice, 'the Doges wed the sea with rings'. At this rate, ten generations could be co-extensive with all the history of the *Serenissima*.

There is a story of an old woman, who lived in Malamocco, in A.D. 810. As a child I was perfectly certain that this must have been my grandmother.

Malamocco is an older town than Venice. It lies at the mouth of the river Brenta, and once held the key to the traffic with Padua and the mainland. At that time, Charlemagne had given the Kingdom of Lombardy to his son Pepin, who made an attempt to incorporate the small island state that bordered on his own dominions. Malamocco, after a stout resistance, was occupied by Pepin's troops, eager for loot. But theirs was a barren victory, for the inhabitants had thrown themselves into their galleys and taken up a position on Rialto. Here they were protected from invasion, not by one canal, but by the lagoons themselves. It is said that Pepin found only one old woman in Malamocco. The Frankish King summoned the refugees on the Rialto islets to surrender at discretion. On their refusal, he asked advice of the old woman as to how to subdue them, and he offered her money. . . . The old woman took the money and advised the King to make bridges of boats. And she assured him that, between Rialto and Malamocco, the water was shallow. This was true enough, but it was not all the truth. The lagoons especially at low tide, are shallow, where the bed is not intersected with the older beds of ancient rivers. And the mud is oozy and treacherous. Unfamiliar as they were with those sheets of water and the action of the tides, many of Pepin's men lost their lives. They made an attempt to seize Rialto with larger vessels, but these were left high and dry by the receding tide. As they lay stranded, the islanders set fire to them. The return of the tide enabled Pepin's shattered fleet to withdraw, but he had to acknowledge himself defeated. He died soon after, in Milan.

Those refugees on the sixty-odd islets of Rialto were the original founders of Venice. And—as I mentioned above—I once believed that my grandmother had been one of them. Her maiden name was Elisabetta Pilon. I remember a portrait of her: an old lady with a fine profile, enhanced by a square linen cap, quite plain, like those that they wear in Holland. (She was the first of three Elisabeths, for my mother's name was Elisabeth, and so is my wife's—though hers has been shortened to Bettina.) The surname of Pilon which my grandmother bore before she married, has a certain fascination. It takes one back to the days when Venice was born by piles driven into the muddy ooze, to lay the first foundations!

Like Rome, Venice began as an asylum city. Refugees from the mainland took refuge on the islets. The first settlers made their homes in rude huts of osier, like swans' nests among the reeds. Foundations on piles came later, and the buildings in that style must have resembled those constructed by the lake-dwellers in Switzerland. The first inhabitants cut ditches to retain the water at low tide and give shelter to their boats. They built palisades of wattled osiers and made bricks out of the mud itself, building their homes along the banks of natural canals. In his *Italienische Reise* Goethe writes:

It was no idle fancy that their colonists fled to these islands; it was no mere whim which impelled those who followed to combine with them; necessity taught them to look for security in a highly disadvantageous situation, which afterwards became most advantageous, enduring them with talent, when the whole northern world was immersed in gloom. Their increase and their wealth were the necessary consequence. New dwellings arose close against dwellings, rocks took the place of sand and marsh, houses sought the sky, being forced, like trees enclosed in a narrow compass, to seek in height what was denied them in breadth. Being niggard of every inch of ground, as having been compressed into a narrow compass, they allowed no more room for the streets than was absolutely necessary for separating one row of houses from another, and affording a narrow way for passengers. Moreover, water was at once street, square, and promenade. The Venetian was forced to become a new creature; and Venice can only be compared with itself.

The first bridges were made of wood, and their inclined planes might be crossed by horses and mules. This left a trace in the name of one of the bells in the Campanile. The bell that used to summon members of the Grand Council to a meeting was called *La Trottiniera*, because the councillors came trotting on their mules to the Doge's Palace. This custom ceased when the bridges began to be made of stone, with steps.

The first merchandise that the Venetians traded in was salt and salted fish, which they exchanged in Carinthia for iron. But soon Venetian ships sailed out of the Adriatic towards the East, and a people grew up, hardy, gallant and adventurous. A new civilization was born, having the same virtues that had been those of the Romans and which, in the distant future, were to inspire the Pilgrim Fathers.

From her first beginnings, Venice claimed independence from both East and West: from the Emperor of the Eastern world, in Byzantium, as from whoever might rule in Italy.

'God, who is our help and our protector, has saved us that we might dwell upon the waters. This Venice, which we have raised in the lagoons, is our mighty habitation; no power of Emperor, or Prince, can touch us!'

Such was the answer given to Flavius Longinus, the representative (exarch) of the Byzantine emperor, who endeavoured to make the Venetians acknowledge themselves as his subjects. The same Longinus admitted that the Venetians were 'indeed a great people with a strong habitation'.

The power and splendour of Venice reached its zenith in the Quattrocento between the years 1400 and 1520. It should be kept in mind, however, that in the year 1453, Constantinople was taken by the Turks, thus creating a formidable enemy for all Europe.

Florence and Milan and Genoa might be wealthy, but it was said, not without truth, that all the gold in Christendom passed through Venetian hands (even though they might be the hands of Shylock!). The Venetian *zecchino,* or golden ducat, circulated round the Mediterranean and as far as Calicut in the Indies. It was known in England, as 'the sequin': stamped with the figure of the Doge, kneeling before St. Mark, or beside the Lion with his paw on an open book.

At one time the English used to send their woollens to be dyed on the Giudecca.

Cloth of gold and of silver; tenuous silken veils, delicate and sparkling as cobwebs on dewy mornings; heavy brocades, damasks and velvets (though cut velvets were a speciality of Genoa)—these were made in Venice, or imported from the East. At the coronation of Richard III, King of England, in

1483, the lace worn by courtiers, great ladies and ecclesiastics, came from Venice. And so did the table glass and the mirrors.

Though up till the French Revolution *et ultra,* most governments were tyrannical, sentimental novelists gloat over the cruel tyranny of the Ten (or the Three), just as they make a pathetic swindle out of the Bridge of Sighs. Yet the *Serenissima* was much regretted by its subjects, when it fell, and no government was better or more willingly served, while it lasted, nor claimed a more rigid honesty in its dependants.

It seems impossible, when you look down on the City from the belfry of the Campanile, to believe that this fugue of russet roofs covered, in A.D. 1250, the most powerful state in the world. Only the wisest and most popular of governments could have achieved so much, with so little.

At the beginning, it proved necessary to curb the power of certain nobles, eager to set up an absolute monarchy, to be hereditary in their own families. Later—in the thirteenth century—it was the power of the lower classes that had to be curbed, for disorders created by them during elections tended to weaken the State, when it needed all its strength for the wars against Genoa (similar, in some ways, to the wars between Rome and Carthage).

The *serrata del Gran Consiglio,* a conservative constitutional reform, made of Venice an Oligarchy, and such it continued to be, till the end. The patricians held the responsibility and the privileges of a governing class, but accompanied by so many duties and obligations, so rigidly enforced, that the upper classes were indeed the servants, as well as the masters, of the community, and unpaid servants at that!

A patrician belonged to the Republic and was trained for service from his early youth. A nobleman of ripe experience and great wealth might be sent abroad on diplomatic missions, and kept away from home, for years, at his own expense. A general, or a sea-captain, was expected to win battles. If he lost them—without sufficient justification—such unlucky commanders might be, and often were, imprisoned. The most notable instance is that of Vettor Pisani, a brave and successful admiral. In the wars against Genoa he won many victories, but he was defeated off Pola by Luciano Doria. For this, the Senate ordered his imprisonment. He was liberated when the City was in great danger. He assumed once more the command of the Venetian fleet (A.D. 1378-80), and made naval history, proving how a superior maritime power, having suffered disaster in home waters, is yet able to win in the end, by holding out till squadrons in distant seas can be recalled for its defence.

The proudest patrician names might be held up for perpetual infamy, if the bearers failed in their duties. In no other country in the world have I seen marble tablets set up in the walls of public edifices, with inscriptions which do not praise, but condemn. You may read them under the arcades of the Doge's Palace, facing the Piazzetta. For example:

MDCLVII—XV FEBBRARO
Girolamo Loredan

e

Giovanni Contarini
furono banditi per l'abbandono della
Fortezza di Tenedo
Lasciata liberamente in mano dei Turchi
con le armi e munitioni pubbliche
con notevole pregiuditio della Cristianità
e della Patria.

meaning that Girolamo Loredan and Giovanni Contarini were banished for having ceded the fortress of Tenedos to the Turks, with its arms and munitions, causing grave injury to Christianity and to their country.

Another tablet tells how Pietro Bontio, a clerk in the Armaments Office, was banished for serious mismanagement of the public moneys that were in his charge.

There was no charitable glossing over unpleasant facts, or white-washing of aristocratic culprits, in the *Serenissima*!

NOTE. Out of the story of Vettor Pisani in the so-called 'War of Chioggia', as told in Venetian chronicles, an English author made a book for boys and girls, called *The Lion of St. Mark's*.

G. A. Henty had been war-correspondent in 1866, following Garibaldi in his campaign in the Alps. Later, he found his real vocation, writing for young people. In this book he told the story of an English boy, brought to Venice by his father at the end of the fourteenth century. He learns to speak Venetian and to row a gondola. He is instrumental—under Pisani—in saving the city from destruction.

Needless to say, he ends by marrying a beautiful Venetian girl—a great heiress—and living with her happily ever after.

3

GHOST OF AN OLD COURTSHIP

Another of the heroic labourers and sufferers for Italian independence and unity, Giovanni Battista Varè, died at one o'clock yesterday morning. During the sixty-seven years of his life, he ran the complete career of an Italian liberal; he once filled high office in a republican assembly; he had to fly his native country and undergo all the hardships of a political exile . . .

The London Times—21st April 1884

THE *Serenissima*, far advanced in its decline, was swept out of existence by Napoleon I and by him handed over to the Hapsburgs, to become part of the Austrian Empire.

In 1848—the year of unsuccessful revolutions throughout Europe—the City had a brief interval of independence. But in August 1849, the victorious general Gorkowski, re-entering Venice at the head of Austrian troops, after a prolonged investment, loaded the Venetians with an even heavier servitude. My father and thirty-nine others, were sent into exile. This exile ceased only when Venice became part of the Italian Kingdom, in 1866.

Four years later, the Franco-Prussian War of 1870, causing the withdrawal from Rome of the French garrison that protected Pope Pius IX from his subjects, gave to the Italians the opportunity to occupy the Eternal City. And in 1871, the first Italian Parliament was opened in the capital of united Italy, by King Victor Emanuel II.

It so happened that my Scottish grandmother, Margaret

Chalmers of Aldbar, and her five daughters—not to mention a female courier called Marie, a small dog and a canary-bird in a cage, arrived at that time in Rome. The era of big, 'ritzy' hotels was not yet, and the party found rooms in the Via Babuino, just off the Piazza di Spagna, at an inn kept by a Frenchman, Monsieur Henri, and his two daughters.

Those were the days when travellers partook of their meals at a *table d'hôtes*: a long table at which they were placed in order of seniority of residence. Among the other guests at Monsieur Henri's *table d'hôtes*, was the newly-elected Deputy of Venice, who had come to the new capital, to represent his native town in the Chamber.

This gentleman—by name Giambattista Varè—had just taken his place at table, when the door of the *salle-à-manger* opened to admit an elderly lady with ringlets and a white cap with streamers that fell down her back. She was followed by an Indian file of daughters, the eldest of which took a chair next to the Deputy from Venice. They were soon in deep animated conversation, carried on in French.

Little more than a year later they became engaged.

In 1874, they were married in St. George's, Hanover Square, London.

It was a union between Scotland and Venice: lochs and lagoons, moors and moorings, pibrochs and barcarolles, cairns and *campanili*, James Barrie watching life through a window in Thrums, and Carlo Goldoni viewing it from the wings of a theatre on Rialto.

* * *

If any of my readers go to Venice, they may notice a bronze medallion on the outer wall of the Square of St. Mark's, as you enter it, coming from San Moise. On the inscription is the same surname that figures on the cover of this book, and others by the present author. I am glad they put up a bronze medallion to my father, representing him in bas-relief, and not a statue, like that of Manin (in what used to be called the Campo San Paternian), in a lapidary frock-coat, with a rather trumpery lion at his feet. The Risorgimento unfortunately flaunts itself in statues and monuments whose incongruity of colour and form is apt to destroy the mellow unity of some old piazza. Such monuments are often utterly unworthy of the heroic figures they propose to commemorate.

In a novel called *Doctor Antonio*, written in English by Giovanni Ruffini (a distant connection and fellow-worker of my father's) tells of an English girl who falls in love with an Italian revolutionary. But the marriage is prevented by her brother. In Mother's case also, objections were raised to her marriage. *Her* brother, Frank Chalmers, did not like the idea at all.

The family attitude was perhaps best expressed by the Aldbar gamekeeper, 'old Bailey', who said he was 'sorry Miss Lily would marry a nigger'.

I never met my Uncle Frank, who died young, but I recognize the type of Scottish 'Laird', in a letter of his, dated 17th March 1870, written from the *Fonda de Londres*, in Seville.

The writer dislikes the Spanish ladies, whom he describes as rather vulgar and idiotic, eating an apple with a knife, and taking an olive with a knife from a friend at the dinner table. He complains of the crowd at the fair and of the prices at the inn (two pounds a day for two people with food). Apparently the 'sights' of Seville interest him very little. What he likes best is that there are some Scottish neighbours there, Lady Airlie and Lord Strathmore. Also a gentleman from Dundee who, however, gives him a distressing piece of news: a fox has been shot on the estate at Aldbar. . . . *Ruat coelum!*

How could a man with such a background and such a mentality approve of his sister marrying 'a rebel', a fellow-conspirator of Mazzini's?

The old courtship comes to life for me in the letters that Mother treasured.

ELISABETTA VARÈ, *NÉE* CHALMERS

CATERINA RUFFINI

GIAMBATTISTA VARÈ

DANIELE MANIN

GIOVANNI BATTISTA VARÈ, 1817-1884. MEDALLION FORMING PART
OF TABLET TO THE AUTHOR'S FATHER, AT THE ENTRANCE TO ST.
MARK'S SQUARE IN VENICE

There is a letter of my father's, dated Venice 17th May 1874, and beginning *Ma chère et bonne Elizabeth*, he mentions a book he had sent her some time before: *Picciola*, a romance by Saintine. The story is about the Count Emile de Charney, who in the times of Napoleon I was imprisoned in the Fortress of Fenestrelle, in Piedmont. This is a castle where once political prisoners were interned, built in the form of a gigantic stairway of fortifications, resembling an illustration by Gustave Doré to Ariosto's *Orlando Furioso*. Successive forts climb up the valley of the Chisone almost to the snow of the High Alps. One mounts from fort to fort by a covered stairway that seems never to end.

There is a whole literature about political prisoners in the nineteenth century, beginning with Silvio Pellico's *Le Mie Prigioni*. Many of these captives save their reason by making friends with some small creature, such as a spider, or a mouse. Charney develops an almost morbid cult for a tiny plant that forces its way between the paving-stones in his prison yard. He tends it and calls it 'Picciola'.

The novel is a masterpiece of that sentimentality that was rampant in the Ottocento, as distinguished from the really deep emotion, the *herrliche Gefühle* that Goethe speaks of in *Faust*. Such sentimentality went out of fashion with the candles that shed their mellow light on people's emotions. Our present-day, glaringly illuminated lives have brought us to exaggerate in an opposite sense. We hide our tenderness under a cloak of sophistication.

My father was a patriot of the Risorgimento. With him and others like him, love of country caused a purification of the emotions, similar to filial love, and it formed crystals of pure sentiment. Like Charney, he had been imprisoned (in Genoa, in 1857) for complicity in insurrectional attempts. This is possibly why *Picciola* was a favourite book of his. It was inevitable that he should give his betrothed a copy and that they should mention it in their correspondence. In the spring of

1874, his fiancée sent him, pressed between the pages of a letter, a flower such as that described by Saintine.

In thanking her for it, he writes:

D'abord je veux vous remercier pour la petite fleur bien connue. Pour mieux la conserver, je l'ai mise dans le volume de Picciola, à la page où l'on commence à parler de Teresa, et où l'auteur écrit: 'Là; où elle va sécher une larme et réveiller un sourire, là est sa place, là son orgueil, là son triomphe.'
C'est un passage qui m'a fait bien réfléchir et bien rêver.

As we get towards the middle of the book, the story of the flower becomes known and the Empress Josephine intercedes for Charney with Napoleon, who remarks cynically that a man who can made such a fool of himself over a small plant cannot be a dangerous conspirator. So the hero is liberated and marries his Teresa.

Saintine ends his romance with an anticlimax, and this is perhaps the happiest touch, at least from a literary point of view. The plant is removed from its precarious position in the prison-yard and taken to Charney's home, where he allows nobody to water it but himself. Alas! A happy domesticity brings forgetfulness. Poor Picciola, unwatered, withers away and dies!

These—in an English translation—are the concluding words of the book: '. . . in all this domestic happiness—all these transports of joy and affection—all the rapture and prosperity brightening the home of the Count and Countess de Charney, PICCIOLA had been forgotten; *La povera Picciola* had died of neglect, unnoticed and unlamented. The appointed task was over. The herb of grace had nothing more to unfold to the happy husband, father, and believer!'

I sometimes wonder if Mother's practical Caledonian mind really appreciated all this pathos as much as my father did. But the book had for her many tender associations; it was a treasured souvenir of her courtship.

I was unaware of this when I came across *Picciola* on the bookshelves, when my father had been dead some ten years, and I was a boy in my early teens. I read it with a mild interest and imprudently lent it to a friend. The friend—as so often happens—went away without returning it.

There's a saying in Italian: *Libro prestato, mezzo perduto.* A book lent is a book half lost. And *Picciola*, bound in white vellum and gold-tooled, had disappeared for ever.

When I discovered how precious that volume had been to Mother, I tried to find another copy, meaning to have it bound as the old one had been. But that first edition was long out of print!

Sunt lacrymae rerum!

Half a century later, in the Tate Gallery, I came across the picture by Martineau, representing the Count de Charney, lying on the flags of the prison-yard at Fenestrelle, tending his precious flower. The sight carried me back, not to the days of the great Napoleon and the man who had conspired against him, but to the ghost of an old courtship.

4

GHOSTS OF MY BOYHOOD

IN the autumn of 1891—my father having died seven years before, and I being eleven years old—Mother and I came back to Italy, after passing several years in England and Scotland. We settled in Rome, but Mother wished me to know, and to keep in touch with, my relations in Venice, so she would take me there at least once a year. We put up in the Hotel Regina, on the Grand Canal. That hotel still exists, but it has become more luxurious and fashionable than it was in the last decade of the nineteenth century.

The first thing I noticed about our family in Venice was that, all together, they filled seven gondolas.

Venetians are gentler in their manners than other Italians; theirs is *la dolce maniera*. As Madame de Lande wrote of them, in a book of travel: '*Ce peuple n'est ni remuant, ni féroce, mais gai, tranquille et facile à contenir.*' In the days when poor Italian emigrants were exploited abroad, the people who made a profit out of them preferred to deal with Venetians, as being more docile than their nationals from other regions in the peninsula.

From the first, I was conscious of a different mentality; and the impression was mutual. Our Venetian connections would have been pleased if Mother and I could have taken up our abode with them, in their native town. As we did not, we remained—or at least I did—something of a puzzle to them. I think they were a little shocked at the way I was brought up, considering it outlandish and bizarre. Possibly they regarded our semi-foreign ménage much as our first ancestors in Venice must have looked upon the Goths and Lombards: semi-barbarous inhabitants of the mainland.

As our visits to Venice were repeated in the passing years, there arose different causes, not of any real incomprehension, but of a mild bewilderment.

The first of these had its origin in a difficulty to understand each other's language. During a prolonged stay in the British Isles, I had partly forgotten my native tongue. On my return home, I first picked up the Roman dialect, *il romanesco*.

Venetians have a language of their own, which it took me a little time to learn. Some of the words resemble French, and they call this 'franco-veneto'. Their language was used officially in the law courts and public offices, even after the fall of the Republic. Venetians have always liked to be sufficient unto themselves, and not to be dependent on the mainland, even culturally. Perhaps this is why they have had no great writers, except Goldoni (and Sarpi, in matters of theology). Most of Goldoni's plays—and the best of them—are in the vernacular.

For those of my readers, who may be interested in philology, I will point out some of the differences in words:

VENETIAN	ITALIAN	ENGLISH
Pistor	*Fornaio*	Baker
Pestrin	*Lattaio*	Milkman
Piron	*Forchetta*	Fork
Carega	*Sedia*	Chair
Avrir (like *ouvrir*)	*Aprire*	To open
Ruga (like *rue*)	*Stradicciola*	Lane
Cavei	*Capelli*	Hair
Squero	*Cantiere*	Shipping-yard

Salizzare (in Italian: *lastricare*) means 'to pave', and *Salizzada* is a paved street. (In ancient times, Venetians walked on grass, or mud, and their wives and daughters wore *zoccoli*, or pattens.)

A word that exists in Venetian and in no other language, is

nonzolo. The *nonzoli* were the retainers of the Papal Nuncio.

Bettina (my wife) tells me that she notices the Venetian cadence in the voices of the children and young people much less now than when she married me in 1909. Can it be that local dialects are dying out? Do they still talk with the cadence of the Lowland Scot, in the streets of Dundee?

Even in their speech, Venetians are more courteous than the Italians of the mainland. This corresponds with what W. D. Howells calls 'their uncostly gentleness of bearing'. And he adds: 'At home, it sometimes seems we are in such a hurry to live and be done with it, that we have no time to be polite.'

After we had got over the language difficulty, other peculiarities (as they appeared to my Venetian relations) served to mark the difference between their outlook on life and ours. On two occasions, when we were in Venice (in 1894 and 1895), Mother had with her a German maid called Agnès. I suppose that the memory of Austrian domination was still fresh in the minds of the elder people, for they disapproved of our having anybody in our household who spoke German. Such a criticism being too unreasonable to merit any attention, they expressed surprise that Agnès should also look after me. What—they asked—did a boy of fifteen want with a *governante*? It was almost improper!

One of my last surviving cousins told me, not long ago, that his parents used to take him, when he was about eight years old, to see Mother and me at the Hotel Regina. He added that he had been perplexed (*'rimasi perplesso'*) by the way I was dressed. And he spoke of a short black jacket and a large turn-down collar. From this description I gather that I must have been wearing an Eton jacket, and that, in all probability, such a garment had never been seen—at least not on an Italian —in Venice before!

To my Venetian relations it had seemed extremely unsuitable.

I don't know what age I may have been at the time: possibly seventeen. And it may also be that I had grown out of that suit. But as long as it was possible for me to get into it at all, Mother's economical mind would never have allowed me to discard it.

*   *   *

Of my father's sisters, one had married a Milosevich and one a Ruffini. Of my first cousins, one had married Bosisio, and one Trevisan. At first I had considerable difficulty in remembering their different names.

My aunt Milosevich lived in a red corner-house, close to the Accademia, overlooking the Campo della Carità and the Grand Canal. From her windows one could watch the people passing over the ugly iron bridge that, for some reason which I did not ascertain, they called 'il ponte inglese'.

If *my* Eton jacket appeared to the cousins as inappropriate to my age, the elder Milosevichs seemed to me to be attired in a costume inappropriate to any age. Obviously, they followed no dictate of fashion, but dressed to please themselves. My aunt had a very small head that surmounted a figure shaped like a bell. Her full skirt, combined with a black Venetian shawl over her shoulders, and a black lace mantilla over her head, produced an inverted-cup-shaped silhouette, which so impressed her nephews and nieces that we used to make drawings of her, in charcoal or pen and ink, and vie with each other in attaining a recognizable likeness.

Day and night, her husband wore what, on the Continent, we call a *frac*, meaning a dress-suit, with an open black waistcoat and a black satin tie (perhaps it would be more correct to call it a cravat). He also sported a top hat made of beaver and—in lieu of an overcoat—a Scotch tartan plaid.

Mother, born and bred in 'Caledonia stern and wild', informed me that the tartan favoured by Uncle Milosevich was that of the Campbells of Breadalbane: light green, crossed over with a darker green; the stripes broad, with an edging of yellow. Later, I noticed various elderly gentlemen of Venice, wearing tartans of the Scottish clans. They bought them on the bridge of the Rialto, in the same shops that sold the *scialeti*: black shawls made of wool, with a silk border, netted, ending in long tassels.

Old Milosevich spoke of these plaids as *Vestiarum Scotorum*. Even as a schoolboy, I could follow what he said better in Latin than in his native Venetian, which—spoken by him— seemed to have abolished all consonants except *x* and *z*.

He always seemed very busy. Being of an enquiring mind, I tried to find out what he did. At first, I understood he was a bone-setter, for he was known in the neighbourhood of San Vio as *Suor Giuseppina acconcia ossi* (Sister Josephine, who mends bones). Why the feminine gender I could not say, except that it sounds, somehow, more affectionate, and old Milosevich was much beloved throughout the *sestriere* of Dorsoduro. But the bones he mended were not human; they were financial. Whenever there was a danger of bankruptcy and the City Fathers, or a monastery, or a convent, got their accounts into a muddle, they would appeal to Giuseppe Milosevich, to make them balance again. He was a kind of chartered accountant. This profession is an ancient one in Venice, since Fra Luca da Borgo, at the end of the sixteenth century, published a treatise on book-keeping, double-entry and methods of conveyance.

In those days, Agnès was teaching me German. She made me read Gustav Freytag's *Soll und Haben*. Because of a certain sturdy middle-class realism, the characters in that novel reminded me of Uncle Milosevich.

Some of his descendants came later to settle in Rome. I have mentioned Elia in my *Ghosts of the Spanish Steps*. He was one of those lightning calculators, one reads of occasionally in the newspapers, and he applied his familiarity with figures to astronomy, ending up as Director of the Observatory in

Rome. His son Federico was, for some time, *Rector Magnificus* of the University. They were a talented family, but queer. I sometimes flatter myself that they thought the same of me.

*   *   *

My father's other sister, Caterina Ruffini, was a widow and lived in the Calle delle Botteghe. This narrow street runs into the Campo Santo Stefano, also called Campo Morosini, because Francesco Morosini, '*il Peloponnesiaco*', had his palace there and is buried in the church of Santo Stefano, under a huge and ornate bronze slab in the paving. Augustus Hare, in his guide-book of Venice says that 'this great Doge distinguished as a general in the defence of Candia and the capture of Athens, deserved a nobler monument! My aunt Caterina, who used to go to Mass in that church, complained that the sculptured bronze of the slab-tomb caused her to stumble. She spoke as if Morosini's ghost ought to emerge and beg her pardon. But Zia Caterina was going blind and could not see where she was walking. Despite this disability, she insisted in going about alone, with the result that she fell twice into the canal near Santa Maria Zobenigo, and came home sopping wet. Such incidents only served to remind her of the days when her father and mother and their children had bathed, in summer-time, from their own front door, shouting greetings to any acquaintance that might pass in a gondola.

The last time Bettina and I were in Venice, we took refuge from a storm by passing an hour in the church of Santo Stefano, while outside the lightning flashed and the thunder rolled interminably. In the portico of the cloister, the rain, collected off the roofs, poured out of the long metal spouts that threw the accumulated water on to a raised quadrangle, round an old marble well-head with a metal top.

Inside the church, I found the same old *prie-Dieu*, where I used to see old Caterina kneeling, near the side-altar dedicated to those employees of the Arsenal, whose job it was to caulk the seams of the ships with tar and oakum. An inscription rendered almost invisible by the passing years runs:

ALTARE ARTIS CALAPHACTORUM NAVALIS MONUMENTUM
ANNO MDCCXXXIII RESTAURATUM

The other inscription, the one on the floor, over which Aunt Caterina used to stumble is:

FRANCISCI MAUROCOENI PELOPONNESIACUS
VENETORUM PRINCIPIS OSSA 1694

The church grew darker, as the afternoon light waned, and though it was still raining and we had no umbrella, Bettina and I at last ventured out again into the Campo Santo Stefano. Just before passing through the side door of the church, I looked back, and it seemed to me that there was another shadow among the shadows. Kneeling at the *prie-Dieu*, was the familiar figure of my father's sister. A touch of white hair showed through the black lace veil; the face was hidden by the white hands, as the old lady prayed.

In good weather, Zia Caterina passed most of her time in a wicker arm-chair on a terrace, overlooking the neighbouring roofs and surrounded by chimneys of the characteristic Venetian shape, topped by what looks like an inverted flower-pot. To reach that terrace, you had to pass through the kitchen. Perhaps this was why a constant companion of my aunt, when she sat there, was a large black cat with green eyes, who went by the name of 'Bepi', short for Giuseppe.

If I believed in the transmigration of souls, I might have thought that Bepi reincarnated the Doge Lorenzo Loredan, whose portrait hangs in the National Gallery in London. There was about him an air of repose and aristocratic calm that must have greatly impressed the lady cats of the vicinity. Had Tennyson known Bepi, he would certainly have added some verses about him in *Lady Clara Vere de Vere*. He was just the sort of cat that might have been hers. At least, in the day-time. But after dark, when all cats are grey, Bepi's behaviour on the roofs was like that of Giacomo Casanova. His was a double personality.

I have often had supper on the terrace with Zia Caterina, and the staple dish was rice, cooked in various ways: with saffron *alla Milanese*, or with periwinkles (*risotto co' i peoci'*) and other 'fruits of the sea'. A local dish was *sguazzetto*, broth with rice in it and bits of meat and chicken, also wisps of vegetables floating about in a way that reminded me uncomfortably of refuse floating out with the tide. But it could be very good indeed.

On the night of some *festa*, the sky might be illuminated with the reflected glare of Bengal lights on the Grand Canal. Sometimes a searchlight on the Campanile would send a luminous shaft that brought to life the gilded statue of Our Lady of Salvation. I seem to remember that, in those days, the statue had been freshly gilded. Now it is green with a patina that is perhaps more attractive.

Zia Caterina's house was plainly furnished and she used the commonest of dinner services—both china and cutlery. Her apartment was without luxuries of any kind, at the top of the house. When I first went there, as a boy, I was disappointed at so much austerity, in a town famed for its magnificence.

After Aunt Caterina had died, her heirs found, in cupboards and chests of drawers, large bundles of bank-notes and bonds, for considerable sums, all dated 1849, the year of the unsuccessful revolt against Austrian rule. Pictures, silver, old furniture, everything marketable had been sold, to acquire the script and the notes—all of which became as worthless as the *assignats* of the French Revolution. Those bonds, bought in our family and by others who sacrificed themselves in the cause of liberty, were issued when in dire straits by Manin's government, of which my father was part.

So it had been in the days of Fichte and of the author of

Undine, during the German struggle for liberty, at the close of the Napoleonic wars. Girls in Berlin had sold their long fair hair 'for King and Fatherland'. Gold rings had been replaced by iron ones, with the inscription '*Gold gab ich für Eisen—1813*'.

In 1849, the young girls of our family had given their earrings.

The pathos of these memories had long been forgotten by the younger generation, at the time when Mother and I stayed at the Hotel Regina. Utilitarian furniture and the absence of pictures and old silver, were not considered a hardship. My cousins belonged to a class of Venetians whose home is out-of-doors, and a dwelling serves merely as a refuge in sickness and bad weather. Home is a place where to pass the night, or part of it, and where to partake of an occasional meal. For receiving company, in the daytime or the evening, there was the Piazza. It was everybody's drawing-room, and you could offer hospitality, or return it, at one or other of the cafés: Quadri's or Florian's, according to the time of day (the sun is on the former's side in the morning and on the latter's in the afternoon).

Aunt Caterina had two sons and several daughters. The eldest son, Piero, built torpedo-boats at la Spezia, thus continuing the tradition of our ancestors, who had built galleys in the Arsenal. The elder daughters, Giannina and Bettina, married and lived in Venice. The second son, 'Nane' (short for Giovanni), and the youngest daughter, Carlina, lived with their mother in the Calle delle Botteghe. These first cousins were older than I; the nearest to my age being Carlina. She must have been twenty-one when I was fifteen, and—like her sisters —she justified the verses in Byron's *Beppo*:

> *They've pretty faces yet, these same Venetians;*
> *Black eyes, arch'd brows, and sweet expressions still.*

Hers was the beauty one finds in portraits of the Venetian school. These Madonnas and Saints are not ascetic, but attractive

young ladies, with rosy cheeks, golden lights in their hair,
and an air of quiet happiness, as if they found the world a
pleasant place to be in.

In the last century, Italian girls were not allowed out alone;
they had to be chaperoned, except perhaps to go marketing in
the immediate neighbourhood of their homes. I was considered
a sufficient chaperone for Carlina, because of my extreme youth
and the fashion of my attire, which—to Venetian eyes—
appeared almost childish! It was also taken for granted that a
boy who was still subject to the authority of a *governante*—as I
was in the first years of our visits to Venice—could not have
eaten of the tree of knowledge. From this slightly abnormal
state of affairs, Carlina and I benefited.

She took me to her heart, Eton jacket and all. In Venice,
she was my guide, philosopher and friend. '*O Beatrice, dolce
guida e cara!*'

We became adepts in the art of *andare per le fodere*: literally
to move about among the linings. This expression signifies to
find one's way, not only by the real *calli*, but by all sorts of
half-hidden passages that have no names, nor deserve any. We
used to push through, like mice behind the wainscoting, under
a confusion of shutters and chimney-flues that jutted overhead,
with an occasional glimpse of green leaves, where some branch
of a tree stretched upwards, seeking the sky.

Carlina ought to have married and had eleven children.
Then I would have idealized her, like Beatrice or Laura, and
imagined her guiding me through Paradise, as she had through
Venice:

> *Vidimi translato*
> *Sol con mia donna a più alta salute.*

But things did not go that way.

Meanwhile I trotted after her contentedly enough, through
the shady narrow streets and the sunny open squares. I was very
different from her brother Nane, who between the ages of

fifteen and eighteen had already been quite the young man about town, or—as they say in Venice—*in Piazza*.

As a rule, poor Carlina must have had a pretty dull time, but she was unaware of the fact, and I doubt she would have preferred a more rackety existence, such as my tom-boy cousins led in Scotland.

One evening, coming from San Maurizio along the Calle dello Spezier, we emerged on the Campo Santo Stefano. Instead of crossing over to the opening of the Calle delle Botteghe, Carlina swerved to the left.

'Aren't you going home?' I asked.

'First I want to show you something that concerns your family.'

'You mean the Varès?' I had always considered our two families as one.

'Yes. Come and look at the stone flags in the pavement.'

There is a chemist's shop just there, called *Farmacia del Milione,* a name that makes one think of Marco Polo. Carlina stopped some ten yards from the shop door and pointed to one of the broad stone flags on the ground. I looked down and perceived a circular indentation.

'That,' said Carlina, 'is where the foot of the cauldron rested, when they concocted the *Theriaca*. Here, as you see, is another hole, and here are two others. The great cauldrons were brought out into the *campo*, opposite the chemist's shop. It was considered a great occasion.'

'That may be, but what is this *theria* . . . , or whatever it was called?'

'*Theriaca*. Surely you know about it?'

'Ought I to . . .? I never heard of it before. Is it good to eat?'

'It was a medicine that was supposed to cure all diseases. It had something like a hundred ingredients, and they used to make it up with great pomp and ceremony.'

'What sort of ceremony?'

'I don't know. I don't think any *Theriaca* has been made since the days of the Republic. But they brewed it under the eyes of the authorities.'

'And what has this got to do with my family?'

'They made it. They owned a pharmacy; either this one or another, on the Rialto. I don't know which. And they specialized in *theriaca*. But our great-uncle, who was a scholar and a mathematician, couldn't be bothered with a shop, even if it brought in money. So he sold it.'

'What a shame!'

'Would you like to keep a chemist's shop?'

'It might be fun. And I'd take you on as my assistant, to do up bottles in white paper and put a little seal on the top. Just think we might start brewing *theriaca* again. Probably, if well advertised, it might become fashionable, and we'd make money hand over fist.'

'In that case, come and I'll introduce you to the chemist. We get our medicines here, so I know him well. Perhaps you might buy the place back some day.'

I followed Carlina and was introduced to an elderly gentleman with sidewhiskers. He was very cordial and showed me some beautiful sculptured panels on the front of an ancient counter. Also old glass and majolica jars on the shelves.

On the second floor of the Rezzonico Palace, now a Museum, they have reconstructed a pharmacy of other days, both inside and out. The original lantern hangs over the door, and a strip of old brick pavement outside serves to complete the restoration. It's a pity they did not show the bronze cauldrons, where the *theriaca* was brewed by my ancestors.

But I don't think *I* would have made a good chemist. I'm too absent-minded. I might try a Dispensary of the Soul: a library like that of Thebes, which Diodorus Siculus describes: ΨΥΧΗΣ ΙΑΤΡΕΙΟΝ.

5

GHOSTS OF MY BOYHOOD
(continued)

Müde war ich geworden, nur immer Gemälde zu sehen
Herrliche Schätze der Kunst, wie sie Venedig Bewahrt.
GOETHE—Venetian Epigrams

MOTHER wished me, while in Venice, to learn something about art and architecture. In this, she was only moderately successful. Like Goethe, I would tire of pictures. From the Madonnas and the Magdalens, I would turn to the beauty of the living face beside me: the face of Carlina, fair as the Virgin in the 'Marriage of Cana'.

In the days of my boyhood, the pontifical Ruskin was supposed to have said the last word in all questions relating to Venetian painting and architecture. The rooms this Messiah had occupied in the Pensione Calcina were still a shrine at which his disciples worshipped. He was quoted in every guide-book. Augustus Hare reprinted pages upon pages of his *Stones of Venice*. The following—about the Basilica of St. Mark's as seen from Bocca di Piazza, is only a short fragment from a much longer extract:

. . . beyond those troops of ordered arches there rises a vision out of the earth, and all the great square seems to have opened from it in a kind of awe, that we may see it far away;—a multitude of pillars and white domes, clustered into a long low pyramid of coloured light; a treasure-heap it seems, partly of gold, and partly of opal and mother-of-pearl, hollowed beneath into five great

BARTOLOMMEO COLLEONI, BY A. VEROCCHIO (See p. 42)

'EXCUSE!' FROM THE PAINTING BY J. M. BARBER

porches, ceiled with fair mosaic, and beset with sculpture of alabaster, clear as amber and delicate as ivory,—sculpture fantastic and involved, of palms and lilies, grapes and pomegranates, and birds clinging and fluttering among the branches, all twined together in an endless network of buds and plumes; and in the midst of it, the solemn forms of angels, sceptered, and robed to the feet, and leaning to each other across the gates, their figures indistinct among the gleaming of the golden ground through the leaves beside them, interrupted and dim, like the morning light as it faded back among the branches of Eden, when first its gates were angel-guarded long ago. . . .

It is a beautiful and a worthy description. Nevertheless, in the days of my first youth, I had a sneaking preference for what Mark Twain had to say about it, in his *Tramps Abroad*:

One lingers about the Cathedral a good deal, in Venice. There is a fascination about it—partly because it is so old, and partly because it is so ugly. . . . Propped on its long row of low thick-legged columns, its back knobbed with domes, it seemed like a vast, warty bug taking a meditative walk.

The picture called 'Pope Alexander III and the Doge Ziani, the Conqueror of the Emperor Barbarossa', is spoken of in *Tramps Abroad* as 'Picture of the Hair Trunk', there being, in fact, a piece of baggage in one corner that might be a large portmanteau, made of some animal skin with the hair outside. Such things were part of a traveller's luggage in the last century, Mark Twain seizes upon this detail and waxes enthusiastic:

So perfect is the Hair Trunk that it moves even persons who ordinarily have no feeling for art. When an Erie baggage-master saw it two years ago, he could hardly keep from checking it; and when a custom's inspector was brought into its presence, he gazed upon it in silent rapture for some moments, then slowly and unconsciously placed one hand behind him with the palm uppermost, and got out his chalk with the other. These facts speak for themselves.

Such gay humour is more instructive than you might think. It inspired Carlina and me to look for what might have been contemporary detail in pictures by Old Masters. And these acquired a new interest. In the picture of the 'Presentation of the Virgin in the Temple' (the one in the Accademia), we found, in the lower corner, an old woman with a basket selling eggs. There is a harpsichord in the background of the 'Supper of Cana', by Alessandro Verotari. In Carpaccio's picture of the Patriarch of Grado exorcising a man possessed of evil spirits, there is a sign hanging on the wall. It represents a sturgeon and was the sign-board of an inn at Rialto. So again, in Bellini's 'Procession', there is the sign-board of the Inn of the Black Hat, close to St. Mark's, where the Club is now, with the entrance in the Calle del Cappello Nero. The inn exists no longer, but it was still there in the days of Ruskin and Augustus Hare: two ghosts that one meets at every turn.

Sometimes in later years, when—alas!—there was no Carlina to keep me company, I continued, all by myself, to play the old game and look for small domestic details in classical pictures. In this I was encouraged by Israel Zangwill, who maintained that the Italians anticipated all Dutch art. In the picture 'The Supper in Emmaus', are plucked geese, meat in the pan, shining copper utensils scattered around, the pot over the glow of the fire, the rows of plates in the kitchen behind. . . .

Thus did the Old Masters paint for us the cosy little realities that inspire an earthy, as well as a spiritual joyousness. And for my part, I go back again with pleasure to Mark Twain's humorous appreciation, as when he speaks of 'Tintoretto's three-acre picture', in the Grand Council Chamber of the Doge's Palace:

> There are ten-thousand figures in it, and they are all doing something. There is a wonderful 'go' in the whole composition. . . . The Lion of St. Mark's is there, with his book; St. Mark is there, with his pen uplifted; he and the Lion are looking each other earnestly in the face, disputing about the way to spell a word—the Lion looks up in wrapt admiration, while St. Mark spells.

A Tramp Abroad and *Innocents Abroad* are a lively commentary on the more serious guide-books, appertaining to the age when every tourist carried a Murray or a Baedeker. Nowadays, they have scant time for reading. The 'lightning-tours' (two days for Rome; one and a half for Florence, and morning-till-evening for Venice) imply at most a guide-lecturer, who instructs them *viva-voce*. When at home, these travellers in motor-buses are mostly hardworking, capable people, and many of them know more about nuclear-physics and such practical matters than we do. In Europe—pressed for time, as they are and breathing fumes of carbon-monoxide—they have to be content with such crumbs of knowledge as fall from the rich men's tables. And they miss the leisurely, quiet thoughtfulness of an old-fashioned *Italienische Reise*. Apart from this, there were travellers in groups even in my young days. Augustus Hare himself might be seen on the Appian Way, instructing a bevy of females that had followed him in landaus. Mother nick-named them 'The Hare and Hounds'.

Sometimes, today, the attention of a group is attracted by objects that are not explained to them by peripatetic lecturers. Once I saw some twenty people, of a northern nationality, staring into a shop-window of an establishment that sold wash-hand-stands and other *oggetti sanitari*. Out of curiosity, I stopped to verify what had drawn their attention: it was an article of plumbing which I understand to be taboo in respectable Anglo-Saxon households!

As with so many other things, sightseeing has become a matter of mass production and of speed. Where once they sauntered, travellers now hurry through streets that their ancestors did not build and where they did not play as children. They glance indiscriminately at palaces, arches and arcades, at rust-coloured houses rising out of the water, at domes and steeples and belfries, floating in a golden glory under a deep blue sky. They plunge into the mystic dimness of old cathedrals and emerge into the sunny glory of an April day. I fear

41

they often miss the real spring that is sweeter than that of Botticelli, the scent of May and the song of thrush and black-bird under a magic tangle of leafy boughs. They know little or nothing of ancient peoples and of great poets: of the Goths and the Goethes! But still, they *do* travel; they *do* see something of it all, and they are content. It may be that theirs is the Kingdom of Heaven.

The lightning tourist, with all his limitations, is more like-able than the over-educated kind. I mean the bickering con-noisseurs who are forever starting quarrels over the attribution of this or that picture to that or this Old Master. These intel-lectual duels grow fiercer as the years go by. They were in full swing during the exhibit in the Doge's Palace of pictures by Giorgione and his contemporaries (summer 1955). There were moments when it seemed doubtful if a Giorgione had really existed. An opposite extreme would seem to argue uncritically that this world of ours was constructed on designs by Michel-angelo. I have a vague suspicion—and if I am wrong, I apolo-gize—that Bernard Berenson is partly responsible for this hyper-aestheticism. His book, *Venetian Painters of the Renais-sance*, was first published when I was a boy of fourteen; but naturally, at the time, I never heard of it.

* * *

One of the narrowest of the narrow streets of Venice is aptly called Calle del Paradiso, recalling the verse in the Gospel according to St. Matthew: 'Strait is the gate and narrow is the way which leadeth unto life, and few there be that find it.'

Carlina found it for me one morning, when we had been to see the equestrian statue of Bartolommeo Colleoni. We emerged into the Campo di Santa Maria Formosa, and when passing in front of the church, she said:

'Come in here a moment. There's a picture I want to show you.'

I was getting tired of churches and pictures and ancient history in general. Nevertheless, I followed her resignedly up the nave to a side altar. Behind and above it was the picture of Santa Barbara by Palma the elder. There was a miniature cannon at her feet, for she is the patron saint of artillerymen. (I wonder what she thinks of the atomic bomb!) The model who posed for that picture is said to have been the painter's own daughter Violante, beloved of Titian. He also painted her, as Flora, and the portrait hangs in the Uffizi at Florence. (I should mention, however, that it is doubtful if Palma Vecchio ever had a daughter!)

As we stopped before the Santa Barbara, Carlina asked shyly: 'Do you see a likeness?'

In the perfect oval of that face there was indeed something familiar, but I could not place the resemblance. I turned an enquiring glance on my companion and was surprised to see that she was blushing. Then I understood. Though her young figure lacked stateliness, there was in Carlina's face something of the calm nobility of the portrait above the altar.

*   *   *

The region known as the Cadore, in the Dolomites, forms a mountain background to Venice, like a drop-scene at the back of a stage. Except for the province of Belluno, it was not then considered as a summer-resort for Venetians. A few days after the Santa Barbara episode, Mother and I went up to Cortina d'Ampezzo, and—at my suggestion—we took Carlina with us.

The first part of the journey was accomplished by rail, and then by carriage over the Austrian frontier. Cortina, at that time, was little more than a mountain village, a cluster of some twenty houses stretching along one street, with the school-house and the church for landmarks. On either side of the broad valley, rose the coral-coloured limestone rocks that are characteristic of the Dolomites.

Some friends and relations of ours were already there, in the Hotel Aquila Nera: the Marchese Alessandro Guiccioli (grandson of the Guiccioli who figures in the Byronic legend), and his wife Olga, née Benckendorff; 'Aunt Isie', otherwise Miss Isabella Inglis—a sister of my Scottish grandmother—complete with sketch-book and ear-trumpet. There was also an elderly gentleman, who appeared to be on intimate terms with the Guicciolis, and whom we got to know through them. We discovered, rather to our astonishment, that he was an Austrian archduke. He had a beard and side-whiskers that stuck out all round his face. This makes me think that he must have been a brother of the Emperor Franz Josef, known in the Hapsburg family as 'Uncle Fuzzy-Wuzzy'. I never heard anyone speak of him except as 'the Archduke', so I don't remember his name.

Apart from these, there were the domestics and two dogs, who had their meals in 'the courier's room'. Mother and I had Agnès. The Guiccioli's had a maid and a valet, called Michele, with side-whiskers that recalled the Archduke's, and the latter had a coachman and a *Jäger* in a grey uniform, piped with dark green. I had Chirillo with me (a Roman *lupetto*) and Olga Guiccioli had a Dachshund called Lumpi, with whom Chirillo had occasional fights.

It was all very rural and restful, as alpine villages were then, before winter-sports contributed to make them fashionable. Mountain streams turned the mills and the hum of those mills joined with the roar of the torrent and the murmur of bees on the meadows. A clean odour of pine sawdust mingled with the fragrance of the pines themselves and of the summer wild flowers. The inn bedrooms were plain and bare, with deal floors, unpolished. Our 'cottage trunks' stood about in the passages or on the staircase landing, there being no room for them elsewhere. The service, by red-cheeked maids in peasant-dress and with plaited hair, was cordial and unsophisticated. In early morning, the song of birds came in through open windows, together with the distant tinkle of cow-bells on the hillside, and chimes from the belfry near-by.

Carlina, who had arrived up there pale with the sultry heat of the lagoons, grew rosy and brighter than I had ever seen her. The elderly Archduke paid her courtly compliments and puzzled her by his affability, she having been taught to consider the Hapsburgs as our oppressors. But it was Aunt Isie, whom his Imperial Highness was most impressed by. He did his best to converse with her, in a rather guttural English, but she had an awkward habit of holding up her ear-trumpet when she herself was talking, and putting it down when it was the other person's turn to speak. This made approaches difficult.

My most vivid recollection of our stay in Cortina is that of a violent thunderstorm in the night. The spire of the village church was struck by lightning, and the crash was terrific. It seemed as if the mountains had fallen and that the hotel must collapse. I heard agitated voices in the passage outside my room, and got up to reconnoitre. Alessandro Guiccioli and the Archduke, both in their nightshirts and wearing nightcaps, were talking anxiously, while their guttering candles, in japanned candle-sticks, spilt the hot wax on the floor. But soon the Archduke's *Jäger* came upstairs with the reassuring news that the harm done was not really serious; only the church was damaged! The scene in the passage reminded me of that described in the *Pickwick Papers*, when Mr. Pickwick, in night attire, gets lost in the dark corridors of the White Horse Inn at Ipswich.

Next morning broke fine and sunny, the meadows sparkling as with a heavy fall of dew. I was standing in the street opposite the hotel, waiting while Chirillo and Lumpi exchanged amenities at the neighbouring corner, with a lot of growling and kicking up the mud with their hind legs. The Archduke was there, discussing with the Guiccioli's valet, Michele, the storm of the previous night.

Aunt Isie appeared in the doorway, with a camp-stool hung over her arm and a sketching-block tucked under her elbow. The Archduke took off his hat and bowed.

'I hope, Miss Inglis,' he said, 'that you were not much alarmed by the storm and the lightning. I hear that one of the church bells has fallen.'

Aunt Isie lifted her face and sniffed with evident pleasure. The keen mountain air was even fresher than usual.

'I think,' she volunteered, 'that it must have rained during the night.'

*　　*　　*

Next year, for some reason which I have forgotten, Mother and I did not go to Venice. When we did so once more, poor Carlina was no longer there.

Something went wrong with her physical health, and this reacted on her brain. The cause may have been a form of anæmia, and perhaps the climate of the lagoons did not suit her.

We were told that she was in the asylum at San Clemente, and we were advised not to go and see her.

I believe that she often spoke of her young cousin Daniele, *il bel cugino*, who someday would come and take her up into the mountains.

She died only a few years ago.

*　　*　　*

Trips such as that to Cortina were part of the yearly peregrinations that Mother never failed to take during my summer holidays. These began in July and ended in October. I sometimes think they were more of a holiday to her than to me, for she liked travelling all the time, whereas I would have been quite content to stay in one place—in the mountains, or by the sea—till we were due to go home again.

Though Mother is buried in Venice—on the island of San Michele—I'm sure her ghost has not its fixed abode there. If it at all resembles Mother, it will not stay anywhere for long. It will haunt trains and steamers and diligences (if it can still find one anywhere). The fuss, the bustle, the small incidents and *contretemps* of the road were as the breath of her nostrils.

Except for the fact that there was no trouble over visas or valuta (even passports were unnecessary), travel was not easy in those days. The railways had few corridor-carriages, and the lighting was by hooded concave lamps in the ceiling, with a residue of oil slopping about in the concave glass beneath them. There were no restaurant cars, and one had to get out to feed hurriedly at the stations, or to have one's luggage examined in custom's sheds at Modane, Chiasso and other frontier towns. Mother made it more hectic than it need have been, by rarely going anywhere direct. She broke the journey wherever it could reasonably, or unreasonably, be broken, making complicated detours to go and see some relation or crony of other days. These might be found anywhere between Aberdeen and Sorrento, Munich and Deauville. It was I who, at times, longed for a little more repose.

Can ghosts travel? I hope so, for Mother's sake. I would like to think she can drive once more up the Maloja pass to the Engadine; thread once more the pine-forests on the coast of the Maremma, breathe the fragrance of lemon-groves at Amalfi; visit the stud-farms and apple-orchards of Normandy, take a little *Dampshiff* down the Rhine.

I imagine her ghost boarding the 7.15 from Euston— some night near the twelfth of August—speeding north through the moon-mantled Midlands, to meet the white glamour of morning, pale over Perth.

CHILDREN AND CATS
AT DORSODURO

NUMBERS on the doorways of the houses in Venice are not those of the single streets, as is customary in other cities. They include all the houses in the quarter, or *sestriere*, of the town, so that the sequence continues through various streets and squares. No. 919 of the Sestriere of Dorsoduro is painted in red figures over a little door opening on the Zattere, that is to say on the broad stone-flagged walk that runs along the Canal of the Giudecca. This canal is so broad and deep that even big ocean-liners can steam down it and disembark passengers and cargo on the street, as on a wharf or pier.

If you go through the door of No. 919, you will find yourself in a cloistered courtyard, whence you can pass into another, vaster court, which is used as a playground for a school: a remarkable school, founded at the beginning of the nineteenth century by the two brothers Cavanis, patricians of Venice and ecclesiastics. They left their fortune, which was a large one, to endow this school. The pupils may belong to any class of society. They pay no fees, but they *must* work. If, through laziness, they make no progress in their studies, they are requested to leave.

When the school is closed for holidays, boys from other institutions sometimes occupy the premises, brought there from the mainland, to enjoy the bathing and other amenities of Venice in summertime.

The first time I succeeded in going to Venice, after the

Second World War, was in 1947. Bettina and I with our daughter Diana, put up at the Pensione Seguso. This has become a home from home for myself and family, since we have no more a house of our own in the City of the Lagoons. The Varès no longer boast of a doorstep on which the seaweed grows. Nor do our mothers feel nervous until the children have learnt to swim.

One hot morning in August, I strolled out to buy the *Gazzettino* at the newspaper stall near the landing-stage of the ferry-boat that goes backwards and forwards between the Zattere and the Giudecca, when I saw a group of boys emerge from the door of No. 919 and run across to embark on a big motor-launch, that was waiting for them. I did not take any notice till one of the boys left the group to caress a large and prosperous-looking tom-cat, who was sunning himself on the steps of the church nearby.

Having bought a paper, I glanced with some amusement at the boy who was keeping his companions waiting and the priest in charge, in order to exchange amenities with a cat. And then I noticed, with a sudden shock of surprise and horror, that the arms held out to caress were mere stumps, without hands. The boys of that group were all *piccoli mutilati* (or *mutilatini*) maimed or blinded in the Second World War, by the explosion of a bomb. Of these bombs, some were the legitimate weapons of modern warfare; others were innocent-looking contrivances, taking various forms, such as a fountain-pen, a toy, or a thermos-flask, so made as to explode and injure anyone who might be tempted to pick them up and handle them.

There were forty-three victims of those booby-traps, who were passing the summer in the school-house of the Cavanis Institute, that has a side-door at No. 919 on the Zattere.

The authorities of the Port of Venice had put the motor-launch *Dalmazia* at the disposal of the *mutilatini*, to take them to bathe on the Lido, or on excursions to Burano, Chioggia, or up the river Brenta on the mainland. In that way, they were passing their summer holidays.

On most mornings, I used to see, from my bedroom window, the *Dalmazia* on its way to fetch the boys for their daily outing; and sometimes in the afternoon, I would go and talk to them after they had got home. Strange to say, the most enthusiastic admirer of the sea was a little boy called Salvatore Gadatella, who had been blinded by the explosion of a mechanical contrivance that, at the same time, had killed his brother. Salvatore spoke of 'seeing' the sea, and he perceived things in the Adriatic that no one else imagined could be there. For example, he saw whales! He was the liveliest of the group and quite unconscious of the terrible scar on his shaven head, where a splinter of steel (so I was told) had severed the optic nerve.

A few days later I met Don Carlo Gnocchi, the priest at whose initiative the boys had been first collected from their homes and cared for at Arosio, near Como. During the war, he had been Lieutenant-Chaplain to a regiment of Alpini ('*la Tridentina*'), mountain soldiers who correspond to the French *Chasseurs des Alpes* and the Austrian *Kaiserjäger*. Don Gnocchi gave me a book, written by himself and called *Cristo con gli Alpini*. They were partly memoirs of the war in Russia.

He had promised more than one dying soldier to look after his children, if he ever got back to Italy, and he regarded this promise as a vow made to God. Get back he did, and as soon as he had recovered from the hardships he had suffered, he went up into the alpine valleys to seek for the families of his old companions in arms. He found many orphans, whom he helped, and he found despairing mothers, whose children had been maimed by booby-traps. He collected these children, and he appealed to the authorities and to the public, for funds wherewith to feed and educate them. No one could have better accomplished the difficult task. Few children could have had a better teacher. Father Gnocchi is an extraordinary man, with an outstanding knowledge of child psychology, which he has gained by practical experience welded to a great love and sound common sense.

It was Christmas time in 1942, when he was in Russia with 68,000 alpine soldiers, making a retreat on the Don, similar in some ways to that of Napoleon's troops on the Boresina, in November 1812. Only 12,000 survived. Don Carlo cannot explain how any of them, himself included, ever reached safety after a calvary of 700 kilometres, in a temperature of forty degrees Centigrade below zero. They were hungry, ill-nourished, often with fever. Every day witnessed savage scenes of starving men fighting over a crust of bread, or a paring of potato-rind—anything they could crunch between their teeth. As they fell by the way, the priest heard their confession and absolved them.

In the summer of 1947, the ghosts of these men seemed to stand round the playground of the Cavanis school in Venice, and watch the children play: the mutilated boys their Chaplain had rescued.

The idea is not all mine. I got it from Alfred Noyes's *The Victory Dance.*

In this poem, the ghosts of the men who died in the First World War stand by the wall of a room where the younger generation are dancing to celebrate the victory. Under the dancing feet are graves.

The maimed boys in the playground are not dancing. They are doing something even more astonishing. They are playing football! ! !

It was entirely their own idea, and the priests who were looking after them were much taken aback. But, of course, they had to acquiesce. A ball was bought, and goals set up.

The boys divided themselves into two teams: those with one leg played against those who had no arms. The result was hilarious. One little boy, who was lame, played while sitting on the shoulders of a much bigger boy, who was almost blind: a collaboration reminiscent of Aesop's fables.

In their life together, the *piccoli mutilati* formed an efficient corporation. Each of them would help to remedy the deficiencies of his companions. They would help each other dress and undress, to eat, drink, and so on.

But their unbringing could not help being a painful one.

'The human body,' Father Gnocchi explained, 'does not grow simultaneously in all its parts. The bones grow quicker than the muscles. When a boy's limb that has been mutilated grows larger, the bone outdistances the flesh, and pressing on it produces inflammation. Every now and then an operation is necessary to regulate the growth of a stump. This may occur three or four times, and is often more alarming to the child than the original accident. I have one boy here, little Bruno, who has suffered much this way. It is heartbreaking to have him on the operating table time after time!'

*　　　*　　　*

I got to know some of the boys quite well, and we had an animated argument about cats.

It was through a cat that my attention had first been drawn to the *piccoli mutilati*, who had many acquaintances among the feline population of the *sestriere*. A mother-cat had established a litter of kittens just inside a doorway leading down to a lumber-room, or cellar, near a corner of the playground. Papà—if indeed he was a relation—could be seen most mornings, performing peculiar and even unseemly toilet operations in the courtyard itself. In these he was sometimes disturbed by the football game. The argument referred to above started between me and a boy called Ambrogino, who had lost the fingers of both hands and one eye. While playing near a well-head in his own courtyard, he had found a pencil, blue at one end and red at the other. He had picked it up and tried to sharpen it, when it promptly exploded. He told me that he was with his sisters when this happened, but they were unhurt.

Ambrogino, and another boy, Vittorino Morè, had noticed, close to the door of No. 919, on the Zattere, a marble slab, or tablet, built into the outer wall, some four feet from the ground. In the centre of this slab is a bas-relief representing a face, round-cheeked and with the mouth open; a sort of letter-box, dating from ancient times and offering to the public a means of denouncing infractions to the rules of hygiene, as laid down, in the days of the *Serenissima*, by the *Magistrato della Sanità*. Accusations and complaints concerning matters of public health were thrust into the marble mouth, just as accusations and complaints of a political nature were put into the more famous 'Bocca di Leone'. This is in the Doge's Palace, and the opening corresponds to the Sala della Bussola, the anteroom of the Council of Ten.

Ambrogino and his companions suggested that I should write a denunciation to put into the open mouth that was there for the purpose, near their hall-door. It was no use explaining to them that nothing could come of it, as the old custom had died out a century and a half before our time. The boys were insistent, and the discussion ended with my complying.

That is to say, I put a sheet of paper into the mouth of the marble face, with the following complaint:

> THERE ARE TOO MANY CATS IN THE
> SESTRIERE OF DORSODURO

signed with my name and address!

The boys however did not agree with what I had written. They had nothing to complain of in the number of the cats. I had to explain my point of view, which was accepted with reservations.

Shylock defined the cats in Venice as 'necessary and harmless'. And I agree. They help keep down the number of rats, which tends to become exuberant on a water-front. But apart from this, Venetians like cats, as they like pigeons. Francesco Morosini (whose tomb in Santo Stefano used to cause my aunt Caterina to stumble) took a favourite cat with him on his galley, when he conquered the Peloponnesus. A less historical figure, by name 'Mosé', belonging to one of the Signorine Seguso, was a well-known character on the Zattere for many years, between the two world wars. I have no doubt that Mosé and Morosini's cat foregather in whatever corresponds, in their afterworld, to meadows of asphodel (possibly the fish-market at Rialto).

But—as I pointed out to Ambrogino and his school-chums—many homeless cats, in Venice, are hard put to it to make a living, and the sight of some miserably thin, ill-nourished pussy, often makes one deplore the mistaken kindness that prevents Venetians from drowning a few kittens out of a litter. There seems to be a superstition to the effect that this brings ill-luck. Fortunately, Venetian children in general, and not only the *mutilatini*, do their best for the cats. There is a *camaraderie* between them.

Bettina (my wife) was much distressed at the sight of a small kitten in a *calle* near San Trovaso, crouching miserably in a corner, and only too obviously starving. While she wondered what she could do about it, a little girl appeared, carrying a large bottle of milk, intended for home consumption. At sight of the kitten, the little girl took off the stopper of the bottle. And she carefully poured almost a tumberful into a small hollow in one of the stone flags of the paving. Thus in the Temple of Vulcan in the Forum, did the Romans pour libations into the hollows of the altar-stone. The kitten then partook of a much needed meal. The child's gesture was spontaneous, and no doubt an habitual one. No danger of being scolded because the bottle of milk no longer contained full measure.

Despite the fact that church mice are proverbially poor, some of the most prosperous, sleek and portly cats seem to belong to the churches. Possibly they feed with the sacristan, or at some neighbouring monastery, where the inmates do themselves well. I have often seen a black and white tabby, asleep on a bench at Santo Stefano, even during Mass, with coloured lights from the stain-glass windows dappling his coat with yellow, blue and crimson.

On the other hand, there is a constant war waged between the gold-braided hotel-porters of the more 'ritzy' hotels and the stray cats who attempt to secure a footing within the establishment. These *concierges* are not always Venetian-born, and local superstitions about cats do not prevent them ordering the bell-boys to throw out such feline aspirants as may succeed in passing through the revolving doors of the hotel.

Smaller hostelries are more hospitable. Between the Pensione Seguso and the Pensione Calcina, next door, there is a tiny lane, called Calle del Pistor, arched over by an outjutting bedroom on the first floor. In that lane, local pussies congregate to receive nutriment thrown to them from the kitchen windows.

The *piccoli mutilati*, with whom I conversed on the subject of cats, were interested to hear that there is in Venice a *Campo delle Gatte*. I discovered it by chance, during my boyish peregrinations with Carlina. It is situated near the church of San Francesco della Vigna. The substantive *gatte* denotes the plural of the feminine gender. Why tom-cats should be excluded is not clear. But it is clear, from the self-important airs of the lady cats in that *campo*, that they consider the compliment paid them as being only their due. It is possible, of course, that . . . *delle gatte* may be a phonetic corruption of . . . *dei Legati* (of the Legates): an allusion to the Papal Nuncios, who had their residence in the vicinity.

* * *

It may be only an idea of mine, but every time I go to Venice, the cats appear to be more numerous than before. Luckily, they don't embalm them, as in ancient Egypt, or there would not be room to bury them even on an island as large as San Michele.

The maimed boys come no more to the Cavanis school-buildings for their summer holiday, nor do the ghosts of our *Alpini* watch them playing football.

I enquired about the *piccoli mutilati* from the porter at No. 919, but he was new to the job, and had never heard of them. Doubtless they have grown and gone out into the world, by ways that harden. Their scars must speak for them still, as Caesar's did, and bear witness to the way war was waged, when they were children.

The last time I heard of Father Gnocchi, he had taken up another mission of mercy, founding institutions for children who are stricken with polio.

Meanwhile, he has written a book called *Restaurazione della Persona Umana*,[1] a philosophy of education and re-education of body, mind and soul. This, for the author, represents an *apologia pro vita sua.*

[1] Published by 'La Scuola' Editrice, in Brescia. Last edition 1950.

7

THE BLIND DOGE

Oh for one hour of blind old Dandolo!
BYRON—*Childe Harold's Pilgrimage*
Canto IV St. 12

Enrico Dandolo was a diplomat, an admiral and a born leader of
men. He was elected Doge of Venice in 1192, when in his eighty-
fifth year, and then founded the colonial empire of the Venetians
in the Near East. Thus Venice became the first great colonial
power in Christian times. Dandolo is buried in the portico of the
church of Santa Sophia in Constantinople: the Basilica that has
become a Mosque. Only a weather-beaten marble tablet records
the date of his death.

The four bronze horses which now adorn the façade of St.
Mark's, were sent to Venice by Dandolo, after the fall of Constantinople.

THIS is how I first began the present chapter. Then it occurred
to me that I was not writing for an encyclopædia.

Let me start afresh, in another way.

It was in the year 1922 that I first took my children, that
is to say Margherita and Diana, to Venice. They were then
eleven and nine years old.

Travelling is supposed to broaden the mind. And it is true
that the two little girls learnt a lot about the pigeons in St.
Mark's, the cakes and ices at Florian's, and the sands and
bathing-huts on the Lido. I tried to teach them also something
of the history of Venice. But here I met with scant success.
Margherita did get as far as to ask what a Doge might be.

But when she learnt that it was not—as she had first supposed—some kind of a rough fox-terrier, she lost interest.

The children had then two grandmothers living, out of whom they got pretty much all they wanted. When I showed them their Italian grandfather's medallion at Bocca di Piazza, they were not impressed. Evidently grandmothers were alive and grandfathers were dead. To have one in bronze was not of much practical use. He couldn't even buy the *Corriere dei Piccoli*, at the newspaper kiosk, across the way.

My next attempt to teach the children a little history was more successful. I wrote a book for them, called *I Voli del Leone Alato*.[1] It's a sort of a fairy-tale. The hero, Marco, is a Venetian boy, who is brought up in Scotland, with his little cousin Dorothea, in a castle called Druimbar.

There is a chapter about Enrico Dandolo. It begins with his funeral and the vigil kept by the Barons of France in the church of Santa Sophia.

Marco and Dorothea stare about them . . .

. . . they found themselves in the nave of a great cathedral, of which the vaulted roof was lost in darkness. And darkness hid the aisles on either side. But in the centre of the church, which was built in the shape of a Greek cross, stood a catafalque surrounded by giant candelabra, bearing painted wax-candles of enormous girth, while from above hung lamps of burnished silver. Lamps and candles gave forth a light that was dazzling in the vicinity of the catafalque, but hardly penetrated into the more distant parts of the church.

Four armed knights stood at the four corners of the catafalque. The cousins could see three of them, the fourth was hidden behind the catafalque itself. They wore suits of chain mail that covered them from head to foot, and above this armour were white surcoats of homespun cloth, with a scarlet cross on the breast. Their steel helmets were flat on top, like cooking-pots upside down.

[1] Published by Bemporad of Florence in 1923, and by Methuen, London, in English, in 1949, with the title: *The Doge's Ring*.

Each knight had leant his lance and shield against the structure behind him, and held his drawn sword, point downwards, resting on the ground, both hands grasping the cross-shaped hilt. The light from above shone on the burnished casques, but the faces of the knights were in shadow. The tall armoured figures, immovable at the four corners of the bier, resembled statues round some princely tomb. . . . The Lion of St. Mark was poised on the top of the catafalque, with head erect and wings outspread.

'I wonder why,' said Dorothea, 'the Lion is up there.'

The nearest of the knights lifted his face and answered: 'It is meet that the Lion of St. Mark should guard the body of a Doge of Venice.'

Marco and Dorothea drew near to the speaker. At the sound of their footsteps, the other knights looked up without speaking, then bent their heads and remained immovable as before. The knight who had answered Dorothea's remark was less taciturn.

'Know ye not,' he said, 'that to-night's vigil was granted to the Barons of France, and none but they should enter?'

The voice was grave, but the knight's eyes were smiling under the steel helm, which, seen from close by, had more than ever the aspect of a cooking-pot. A 'nasal', or short bar, descended to protect the nose, and it might have been taken for a handle.

Dorothea parried the question with another: 'Why to the Barons of France, if the Doge was Venetian?'

'Because he brought us here on Venetian galleys, first to Zara, and then to Constantinople.'

'I thought,' said Dorothea, 'that the Crusades were to liberate Jerusalem. What are you doing in Constantinople?'

The knight appeared taken aback, but after a moment he smiled again, and exclaimed:

'How often have I heard that said by weary and disappointed men! And, now that the Doge is no more, I sometimes ask myself the same question. Philip of Swabia wanted to oppose the Pope's Guelph crusade with a Ghibelline one of his own. It is wonderful what a lot of quarrelling goes on among allies! Each wants to deflect the water to his own mill. This time, it was the crusade that was diverted. The Venetians, of course, were only too pleased to attack the Emperor of Byzantium, the usurper Alexius, who was unfriendly to them. And it is true, of course, that these Greeks were allies of the saracen.'

He was silent a moment and then added: 'The Doge has been the leading spirit of the enterprise up till the very day of his death, though he was ninety years old and blind.'

'Blind!' exclaimed Dorothea.

'Yes, from a wound in the head he received years ago. He had beautiful blue eyes and it seemed impossible that he should be sightless. He moved his ships like a good chess player, who need not look at the board.'

'How was it he came with you?' asked Marco.

'I will tell you. But first you must know that we, the Barons of France, decided on this crusade, after Fulke of Nueillie had preached in our lands, promising plenary absolution to all who took up arms in the service of God for the space of one year. I heard him preach. It was not the promise of remittance of sins that moved my heart and inspired me to take the sign of the Cross. He showed us a picture of Christ's Sepulchre, defiled by the horses of the paynim, and he spoke of the bitter shame that so holy a spot should have fallen into the hands of infidels. It seemed to me that, if I could kneel and pray before the Holy Sepulchre itself, all my sorrows would be lifted and Paradise mine indeed!

'So it came about that I, Geoffroi de Villehardouin, took the sign of the Cross, and with me the two nephews of the King of France: Thebault, Count of Champagne, Louis, Count of Blois, and many others. Later we were joined by the most puissant Baron of the Kingdom, Baldwin of Flanders, whom now we have elected Emperor, here in Constantinople.

'We began by holding a parliament in Soissons. But it was easier to take an oath than to free the Holy Land. It was decided to give letters patent to six knights, who were to visit the sea-ports in search of ships. I was one of the six, and of common accord we went to Venice, where more ships are to be found than in any other part of the world.

'The Doge, Enrico Dandolo, whose dead body we are guarding, was a brave and a wise man. To him we presented the letters patent, in which it was written that all we might stipulate would be held good and approved by the Barons of France. The Doge received us, seated on his throne, wearing a mantle of cloth of gold, and with a golden cap upon his head. Round him were forty-six patricians of Venice, in robes of silk and brocade, most beautiful to behold. This is how we set forth our message:

' "O Sire, we come to thee on the part of the high Barons of France, who have taken the sign of the Cross, to avenge the shame of Jesus Christ and, if God wills, to reconquer Jerusalem. And whereas we know that no people hath more power to help us than thyself and thy people, we beg of you to have pity on the Holy Land beyond the seas, and the shame of Jesus Christ, so that you may take pains to help us with ships and with provisions."

'The Doge considered the matter with his Council, and after eight days they consented to provide us with covered barges, to transport 4,500 horses and 9,000 esquires, besides vessels of war to carry 4,500 knights and 20,000 men-at-arms. And this at the price of four marks each horse and two marks each man. Besides which, the Republic of Venice would, for the love of God, furnish us with fifty galleys fully armed, on condition that, of every capture made on land and sea, Venice should have half.

'After having signed the Covenant, we departed for France, to muster our people and bring them to Venice. This took time, so that we did not return again till Whitsuntide of the following year, which was the year 1201 of our Lord. The ships were ready, and the galleys surged at their warps in the Canal of the Giudecca. But, alas! Not all our kinsmen remained true to their word. Many separated themselves from us and went to embark in other ports. Many turned faint-hearted and refused to leave their wives and children.

'So it came about that, being less in number than we had foreseen, we had not sufficient money to pay the 85,000, as arranged. Therefore we were in great anxiety, not knowing what to do. But the Doge found a way out of the difficulty. In exchange for our help in recapturing the town of Zara, that had been taken from the Venetians by the King of Hungary, he freed us from our bond. And he did more. In the church of St. Mark's, speaking before the people, this blind old man offered to come with us, if we would have him. And we accepted with shouts of joy. Then he knelt before the altar, while they sewed the symbol of the Cross on his hat, so that all might know that the Doge of Venice had become a Crusader. Many others did likewise, for they had faith in his leadership.

'Thus it was every time our courage failed us and we gave up hope, by reason of the many difficulties that beset us and of the quarrels that broke out among ourselves. The Doge was always confident, always quietly determined, always ready to allay our fears, to calm our anger and to remind us of the glorious goal that we were likely to lose sight of, among the daily anxieties and privations. It was enough to approach him and to remain in his presence a little while, for the most timid to feel reassured. It was as if he were the Seer, and we were blind.

'I remember one day in the harbour of Zara, when French and Venetians, forgetting they were allies, fought in the streets of the town, leaving many dead and dying on either side. We were sad also, because some of our most powerful knights, weary of the long quest, had left us and returned to their homes. Of these, one was a Teutonic knight, Werner of Borland, a man of gigantic stature and great strength. He and his retainers departed for their own land, despite their sacred oath.

'The day after his departure, I and some other Barons were at table with the Doge, on the deck of his galleon. We were sad and downhearted, though he had set before us mighty flagons of rare wine. There we sat silent, heaving deep sighs.

'The land breeze gently moved the war-standard that floated above us. Venetian ladies had embroidered it in scarlet and gold. Seagulls circled among the halyards and dipped to the water with shrill cries, every time some scullion from the kitchen threw scraps of food over the side.

'From the shore there came to us, mingled with other noises of the busy port, a sound as of rapid hammering: tac-tac-tàc. . . . The Doge lifted his head and looked, or appeared to look, in that direction. Then he rose to his feet and stood for a while as if to hear better. He wore armour and a broad-brimmed hat, to protect his eyes from the sun. His feet were encased in leather slippers, such as they wear in the East. On days of rough weather, I have seen him go barefoot about the ship, lest he should fall on the slippery decks.

'After a moment he came back to sit among us. "There are storks on shore," he said. "They make that noise with their beaks, tapping the mandibles together, much as a man claps his hands."

'None of us answered. What did we care about the storks? But the Doge continued talking about them, in that quiet voice of his, with its gentle Venetian cadence.

' "When I was a boy," he said, "and sailed into one or other of these ports, I used to get up at dawn to watch the storks teaching their young to fly. The parent storks do so at the beginning, but later they send their children to school, much as we do. Two elder storks, or perhaps three, will teach twelve or even fifteen young ones, who could not all be children of theirs. You will see them in the early morning, manœuvring in long lines, with an elder stork at each end, or else in figures like the letter V, or an arrow's head: the young storks forming the lines and the elder ones at the extremities. They signal to one another and give orders by tapping their beaks, to make the noise we heard a moment ago."

'As we Barons listened to the description of the bird's habit we began to forget our sadness. We had noticed the storks on shore, standing on one leg on their nests, which were placed in the most conspicuous places, on roofs, or on high walls. The Doge chattered on, as old men do, when they become garrulous over memories of their youth.

' "What surprised me most," he went on, "was the indifference with which they sacrificed their young. Each pair of storks, when it builds, or comes back to its next in the spring, has three eggs, which are hatched in due course. Some weeks later, one is aware of a great commotion up on the roofs. The parent storks seem to be having heated family arguments. If you watch them, to see what it is all about, you may realise that Papà Stork and Mammà Stork are busy weighing their young. They lift them and put them down and push them and quarrel over them, till one of the little storks comes hurtling down to earth. After which no one bothers about him any more.

' "I noticed that it was always the largest of the young birds birds that was sacrificed by his parents, and this fact enabled me to solve the mystery of the strange action, so contrary to paternal and maternal instinct. You must know that, in autumn, the storks emigrate. They leave these parts and go to Algiers, to Egypt and to the Holy Land. And they have to cross the sea. But the young birds are not yet strong enough to make so long a flight, so they rest occasionally on the shoulders of their parents.

' "As long as there are not more than two children, all goes well. But if there were three, the parents would not have sufficient strength to help them all on their way. It is a great strain for the elder birds to have to carry the young ones, even for only a few miles. They can manage one each, but not more. Therefore, in anticipation of the long flight, they sacrifice one of their offspring before it begins to fly. And they are careful to choose the heaviest."

'The Doge was silent for a moment, and then added, as if in conclusion:

' "I was thinking of the storks, when you were lamenting the departure of Werner of Borland. It makes me sad to lose such a giant. But perhaps it is just as well for me that I am freed from the heaviest of my young folk, for when autumn comes, I must carry you over the sea, to the Holy Land." '

*   *   *

The years of Enrico Dandolo and the Fourth Crusade mark the highest point in the history of Venice. They brought new riches, prestige and power, but also new liabilities. Increased naval and military forces and the newly acquired Eastern possessions, caused an increased need for supplies of food and raw materials. Venice needed also free access to her Western markets, to dispose of the goods brought from the East. But the exactions of the Carrara family in Padua, and those of the Scaligeri of Verona, crippled Venetian trade with the tithes imposed on merchandise in transit. These great families had to be, and were, eliminated as being no better than robber barons. Thus began the expansion of Venice on Italian Terra Ferma, as far as the mountains.

But by setting foot on the mainland, Venice began to rank

among the Italian States, entering a system of purely Italian politics and becoming embroiled in petty rivalries.

Another danger arose in the East with the destruction of the old Greek empire and its substitution with a weaker Latin one. Thus the way was paved for Mahomedan invasions and the fall of Constantinople to the Turks in 1453.

Such distant after-effects of his achievements do not diminish Dandolo's contemporary glory. He was wise in his generation.

On his portrait in the Doge's Palace is a scroll with the so-called *titulus*, an appreciation of his merits—*Henrico Duci est titulus: Quartae partis & dimidiae totius Imperii Romaniae Dominatoris*—an allusion to the part assigned to Venice of what was then called the Empire of Romania.

No other patrician more worthily impersonates his caste, though many come near it. His ghost should take precedence of all others on Rialto.

He lived in the Middle Ages, sometimes called 'the Dark Ages', extending from the fall of the Roman Empire to the radiant blossoming of the Renaissance. But an age is not 'dark' in which Christianity (even admitting a lay motive) can gather itself together in a common cause and carry the flag of its faith to the grave of its Redeemer.

If the age of the Crusades, of chivalry and the troubadours, of Dante and Charlemagne and Roland, deserves to be called 'dark', then the Renaissance was but an ephemeral flowering, and we live in the Dark Ages still!

8

THE 'DIVINE' PAINTER

Two generations of men had he already seen pass away,
who with him had been born and bred in sacred Pylos, and
among the third generation he held rule.

HOMER—*The Iliad* (1—250—speaking of Nestor)

ON a cold night at the end of January 1505, the Fondaco dei
Tedeschi overlooking the Grand Canal, near the bridge of the
Rialto, on the side of San Bartolommeo, caught fire and was
almost utterly destroyed. Not even a heavy fall of rain in the
first hours of the morning (though attributed to St. Mark's
kind intervention) sufficed to prevent the spread of the
conflagration. A large crowd choked the narrow *calli* and the
two *rive*, as well as the bridge near-by, and hindered the work
of salvaging what might have been brought out and carried
away.

The Fondaco (or 'Fondego', as the Venetians called it) was
the German Merchants' Hall, a combined business-centre and
warehouse. Its destruction was a major disaster, not only for
the Teutonic merchants directly concerned. Almost too many
people volunteered to help. The patrician Bernardo Barbarigo
brought his retainers to form a chain and pass buckets of
water. Two young painters joined in the good work. Barbarigo
recognized them and said: 'From such a calamity only the
architects, and painters like yourselves can make a profit'.

One of the two young men was generally known as Zorzo,
or Zorzòn. He hailed from Castelfranco Veneto, a small town
between Venice and Treviso. We now speak of him as

'Giorgione'. The other came from Pieve di Cadore, in the Carnic Alps, near Belluno. It's a lovely little town, standing on a hillside, high above the green and blue waters of the river Piave. Both painters had been born in the year 1477, but Giorgione had already acquired considerable fame. Salomon Reinach in one of his lectures at the Sorbonne (collected in the volume called *Apollo*) wrote:

> . . . *à Venise, depuis Giorgione, c'est la peinture même qui semble parfois moins préoccupée des objets qu'elle représente, que de l'atmosphère où ils baignent, de la lumière qui les pénètre et les enveloppe. Les Vénitiens n'ont pas été seulement des coloristes, mais des luministes.*

Beautiful bodies, splendid raiment, with the sunlit background of a smiling countryside, gave the impression of a life that was radiant and joyous.

Those were artists in whose paintings one could almost feel the atmosphere, as compared to artists in whose works one merely perceives the stroke of the brush.

But I was forgetting to mention that the other young man— the one who came from Pieve di Cadore—was called Tiziano Vecelli, or Titian.

Barbarigo had been right about those who might profit from the burning of the Fondaco. Following a decree of the Senate, a new building was to replace the old, and Giorgione was commissioned to execute the frescoes on the outer walls. Titian was associated with him in the work, but whereas Giorgione decorated the façade of the edifice (it's the one where the central post-office is now) Titian had the sides to do, with not much space in front of them. Some of the cartoons for these frescoes—both Giorgione's and Titian's—were exhibited in the Doge's Palace in the summer of 1955. A certain superiority of Titian's work is apparent in the cartoons (though they are small, as are Leonardo's in the Louvre) and must have been even more evident in the original paintings, that have long faded out. The contemporaries of the two painters made no mystery of their preference for the *Cadorino* (as Titian was sometimes called), and this rankled in the heart of his partner. The two had been great friends, as fellow-apprentices in the *bottega*, or workshop, of Giovanni Bellini. But now Giorgione refused to have Titian any more in his house.

Ill feeling among the Old Masters was the rule rather than the exception. Another eminent painter of those years, Pordenone, whose style was influenced by Giorgione, was at daggers drawn with Titian, or pretended to be so. While at work at some frescoes in the cloister of Santo Stefano, he ostentatiously went armed to the teeth. . . . Possibly, a form of publicity . . . *pour épater le bourgeois.*

Apart from such adjuncts to his name as 'Cadorino', or 'da Cadore', Titian was sometimes called 'il Divino'. This hyperbole has been confirmed by modern appreciation. The general verdict is that he is the greatest of painters, considered technically. Yet, unlike some recent painters, he never strove to startle, never showed eccentricities, but painted in a straight-forward manner. His works of art are of a uniform excellence, yet avoid the monotony of a dead-level output.

Apart from his soaring genius, Titian got the better of all his contemporaries, by outliving them. Giorgione died in 1510, Carpaccio in 1525, Palma the Elder in 1528, Pordenone in 1539, Michelangelo in 1564. Only Tintoretto survived his former master, and Veronese, who was fifty years his junior.

Titian was the Nestor of artists. He might have lived to be a hundred, if he had not been carried off by the plague at the age of ninety-nine! And he worked to the end, in a sort of *crescendo*, though his eyes watered, so that he had to wipe them continually with *pezze*, little bits of linen prepared for him by his women-folk. It was said of him that his pictures were numberless, like the stars in heaven!

The century Titian lived in—the sixteenth—was compared by Voltaire to a robe of silk and gold, bespattered with blood.

It brought forth many great men, and many of these were painters. The portraits they were commissioned to execute by kings, queens, emperors and other grandees, are often monuments to the artists, rather than to the monarchs whose effigies they have handed down to posterity. The painters conceded to their sitters part of their own immortality. Francis I of France owes a big debt to the artists who contributed to the glory of his reign, so much so that his nationals call him the King of the Renaissance.

In Victor Duruy's *Histoire de France*, I find the following phrase: '*Le prince qui ramassait le pinceau du Titien aimait les arts comme celui qui appelait Leonard de Vinci son père.*'

The prince who is supposed to have picked up the paintbrush that Titian had dropped was the Emperor Charles V (of Spain and Austria). The prince who called Leonardo his father was Francis I.

These legends illustrate the honour in which painters were held in the years when the two rival powers on the Continent (the Hapsburg Empire and France) faced each other in four successive wars.

Titian has made the contending monarchs live for us in his pictures. Their different characters are well brought out. The profile of Francis (the picture is now in the Louvre) shows him with a long nose, but good-looking in spite of it—jovial, unstable, opulent and clever, a king who was as popular with his people as Henri IV, at a later date. The portraits of Charles V reveal him as reserved, tenacious, and prudent. He wears armour, or is dressed all in black, with the order of the Golden Fleece as his only ornament.

*   *   *

Charles V and the Pope Clement VII (Giulio de' Medici) met in Bologna in 1530, and Titian attended the meeting. He was commissioned to paint an equestrian portrait of the Emperor.

This portrait—in which Charles was represented on a white horse—is now lost. But another equestrian portrait supposed to represent the Emperor at the battle of Mühlberg, was painted by the same artist, in 1548. By that time, the sitter was too much a victim to gout to permit his mounting into a saddle. Titian attended him daily in Augsburg, the Bavarian town that takes its name from Augustus. It was the centre of those powerful merchant-princes, bankers to the Hapsburgs, the Fuggers. The Fugger-Haus in Augsburg was painted all over the façade with frescoes, as were so many palaces in Venice, where the Fuggers also possessed a residence. Titian was welcome among them in both towns; old Jacob Fugger was his friend.

The painter had been ennobled by Charles V. He was now a count-palatine (his patent of nobility is still kept in the little Museum at Pieve di Cadore). This empowered him to legitimize the offspring of persons below baronial rank. Around him was an atmosphere of merchant riches, not dissimilar, in some ways, to that of Venice, where patricians carried on the city's trade.

Titian was again in Augsburg two years later (1550) and painted a portrait of Philip II, the Emperor's son. This was sent to England and proved useful in furthering the suit of the prince for the hand of Mary Tudor.

The biographers of great artists, such as Titian, Leonardo, Holbein and Rubens, show how intimately they participated in the national life of their countries and in the international life of their times. They were part of the life that centred round the cathedral, the palace and the castle.

The art treasures they created were often enjoyed—in Italy, at least—by the masses, as well as by the Magnificos. For example, Titian's portrait of Charles V, painted at Bologna, was exhibited to the people, under a portico in the centre of the town.

* * *

Titian's private life had its joys and its sorrows. His young wife, Cecilia, died in childbirth, leaving him with three children. To help him manage his household, his unmarried sister, Orsa, left her home in Pieve di Cadore and came to live with him in Venice. His eldest son, Pomponio, who went into holy orders, turned out a ne'er-do-well, but his second son, Orazio, was a comfort to him in his old age. His beautiful daughter, Lavinia, was the apple of his eye. She married Cornelio Sarcinelli, and—like her mother—died in childbirth after six years of marriage.

Enjoying European fame and great wealth and being the official painter of the *Serenissima*, Titian nevertheless was obliged to write continual dunning letters for payment of the pictures his royal sitters had commissioned, as for the pensions they had assigned him.

He was a man of handsome presence, with an air of penetrating observation and of self-possessed composure. The best of his self-portraits is in the character of Sant 'Ulfo, in the Museo del Prado in Madrid. In the same gallery there is another self-portrait, in advanced age. He was not a man of universal genius and versatility, as Leonardo was, or Michelangelo. His one supreme endowment was that of painting, and every painter can learn something from his technique. His powers remained unimpaired till the end. Even though his eyes watered, his hand never failed him.

What can the life of such a man have been, in his later years? The contemporaries of his youth and middle age had passed away. His mainstay was his son, Orazio, who is chiefly memorable for the attempt made on his life, by one Leoni, when he had gone to Milan to fetch some moneys owed to his father by the Emperor. Father and son lived in a house Titian had taken after Cecilia died, in a locality called Birri Grande, on the Fondamenta Nuove. When not working, the old man would sit in the garden, and let his thoughts ride through the Past, in a long cavalcade of memories. And what did he remember?

His father's house at Pieve, with an outside stairway running up to the first floor, above the stables, and the huge fireplace, and the wood-stack at the back where, he had climbed and played games of make-believe, with his brother, sister Orsa, and the children of the Count of Spilimbergo, who were their friends. One of them was Irene, to whom, years later, he gave drawing-lessons. What merry rambles they used to have together, on the hillsides, in summer woods and winter snow!

His arrival in Venice, with his brother Francesco, to stay in the house of Uncle Antonio Vecellio, an engineer of the Republic. His wife, Aunt Daria, had beautiful auburn hair, and she used to sit on the *altana*, a small wooden terrace above the tiled roof, where the washing was put out to dry. She would comb her hair in the midday sun, to bring out the golden lights in it.

Giovanni Bellini's workshop, and his fellow-apprentice, young Zorzòn. What friends they had been, at first! On the evening of the first of January 1500, they had supped together and boasted that this new century would be theirs!

Then his visit to the court of Ferrara, as guest of the Duke of Este, who had recently married Lucrezia Borgia. She was expecting a baby and not looking her best.

The meeting between Pope and Emperor at Bologna, and the rivalries among the younger members of their retinues, for the favours of great ladies of easy morals.

His visit to France, where a brilliant era was just beginning, an era of splendour, of wit and culture, of laughter and gaiety. And the King's saying that a court without beautiful women was *comme une année sans printemps et un printemps sans roses!*

His visits to Augsburg and the Court there—part Spanish, part Flemish and part German. The homage of the burghers who kissed his hand, and of their good wives who curtsied. The room in the Fugger-Haus, where the Emperor received and sat for him (his foot on a stool). It was warmed with a fire of cinnamon-wood, that Jacob Fugger once lighted—to

Charles's surprise and delight—with an imperial bond for the money owed by him to the firm.

Pleasant home-comings to Pieve, where he was revered as a benefactor of his native village, and peasants knelt as he passed. There was the time he had brought Cecilia back from there to Venice, together with the household linen and plate. She had borne him children, and then he had married her on a sudden impulse, and painted her as a Madonna, with a baby in her arms, for the *Pala di Casa Pesaro*, now in the church of the Frari. She had died, in the summer heat, grasping his hand in her despair. . . .

His daughter Lavinia's marriage, and the gold he had dowered her with, like the rain of gold in the picture of Danae. Almost on the same day, Philip of Spain had married Mary of England. The portrait he had painted of the bride-groom had been, perhaps, too flattering. And that other picture of his, commissioned by the Emperor, when he was about to abdicate: a picture of the 'Gloria'—a sort of apotheosis. The old monarch had hung it in his room at Yuste, in Estremadura, where he died.

Charles had always been a good friend. He had not been easy to paint. The protruding lower jaw and the almost cadaverous paleness were redeemed by the fine brow and the bright, speaking eyes. He had a good figure, and great dignity. 'Most painters,' he once said of himself, 'make me uglier than I am, so when people meet me they are agreeably surprised.'

Titian's friends of the later years had been red-headed Sansovino, who as an architect was so jealous of Michelangelo. And that scurrilous genius, Pietro Aretino (of whom also he had painted a portrait). Aretino's monkey, Monticchio, would imitate Titian at his easel, and was convinced that he could paint as well as anybody!

Poor Aretino! He called himself 'the scourge of Princes' and boasted that the most puissant monarchs feared him, lest he should satirize them in his poems. Certainly they loaded him with rich presents, for no very obvious reason, unless it was because they enjoyed his ribald stories.

Was it really true—the old man wondered, as he sat in the sun, in his garden, where bees were humming in the lilac— was it true that poor Pietro's death had been caused by his falling backwards in his big chair, in a fit of laughter at some disgraceful story, about his own sister?

And then the visit of Henri III, last of the Valois, who stopped in Venice on his way from Warsaw, having fled from there by night, because he preferred being King of France to King of Poland! How cordial he had been, as he walked with the painter in this same garden, under the trees that figure in so many pictures. He had enquired the names of flowers that were unknown to him. . . . On that day, the artist-host— Count Palatine and knight of the Golden Spur—had worn round his neck the heavy gold chain that the Emperor had given him in Augsburg. He had stood by the landing steps, as his royal guest moved off, and Henri had waved his hand to him, as the gondola was about to disappear round the bend of the Sacca della Misericordia.

*   *   *

After Titian's death and that of Orazio, struck down at the same time by the plague, the sumptuous house of Birri Grande was plundered by thieves, who—as happens in times of these disasters—prowled about uncontrolled. They entered the house before the dying man drew his last breath, and he may have perceived their masked faces around him, carrying off his belongings, together with the contagion.

9

MERCHANTS OF VENICE

What, they lived once thus in Venice
Where the merchants were the kings,
Where St. Mark's is, where the Doges
Used to wed the sea with rings?

BROWNING—*A toccata of Galuppi's*

I DO not think that any of my Venetian countrymen, in the days of the *Serenissima*, would have tried to reach the North Pole, like Nansen did, or Peary.

Niccolò Zeno, a patrician of Venice, is reported to have made a long journey in northern latitudes: to have reached Iceland, Greenland and even Labrador (or the 'Vinland' described by Leif Ericcson). But this report would appear to be unfounded, or at least much exaggerated.

It is however perfectly true what Hakluyt says of Sebastiano Cabote: *Scrutatus est oras glaciales Sebastianus quidam Cabotus, genere Venetus . . .,* but *he* was looking for the north-west passage, and incidentally claimed Newfoundland (The New Found Land) for Henry VII of England, who paid him seven pounds for it.

Venetians would have been very much astonished if anyone had described them as 'explorers'. They were merchant-navigators, born of a mercantile aristocracy, out to discover the wealth of nations and to exchange one thing for another: a propensity which—as Adam Smith pointed out—is common to all men and to be found in no other race of animals.

Being a bit of a wanderer myself, I am more familiar with the peripatetic ghosts of the Rialto, than with the more sedentary ones.

The ghosts of the three Polos—Maffeo (the eldest), Noccolò and Marco his son—are those with whom I am most intimate; especially with Marco. We met, not in Venice itself, but in the far countries which are described in the famous book of travels: in the northern deserts of Asia; on the upper reaches of the Yangtzekiang, on what is now the Burma road (it was merely a path, even in my time), in Canton, in Ceylon, and so forth and so on. . . . I used to get annoyed at not being able to go anywhere, except America, without the Polos having been there before me.

To his contemporaries, the tales told by Marco Polo must have seemed like bits out of the *Arabian Nights*.[1] But modern travellers in Asia agree that his descriptions of this place or that correspond to their own observations and experiences. As Colonel Yule says in the first paragraph of *Marco Polo and his Book*: 'It is a great book full of puzzles, whilst our confidence in the man's veracity is such that we feel certain every puzzle has a solution.'

Where a discrepancy is noticeable, it often comes from a confusion in names, or in some material error in longitude. This is so (I believe) in the case of the Desert of Lop.

I quote from Marco Polo:

ON THE CITY OF LOP AND THE GREAT DESERT

Lop is a large town at the edge of the Desert which is called the Desert of Lop, and is situated between east and north-east (*tra levante e greco*). It belongs to the Great Khan, and the people worship Mahomet. Now, such persons as propose to cross the Desert take a week's rest in this town to refresh themselves and their cattle; and then they make ready for the journey, taking with them a

---

[1] . . . *Gelangen wir aber auch nicht sogleich über das Einzelne zur Deutlichkeit, so ist doch der gedrängte Vortrag dieses weitausgreifenden Wanderers höchst geschickt, das Gefühl des Unendlichen, Ungeheuren in uns aufzuregen.*

Dabei das ganze Jahr Geschenke ausgespendet und empfangen. Gold und Silber; Juwelen, Perlen, alle Arten von Kostbarkeiten im Besitz des Fürsten und seiner Begünstigten, indessen sich die übrigen Millionen von Untertanen wechselseitig mit einer Scheinmünze abzufinden haben.

Goethe on Marco Polo in the *Westöstlicher Diwan* (Collected Works).

month's supply for man and beast. On quitting this city they enter the Desert.

The length of this Desert is so great that 'tis said it would take a year and more to ride from one end of it to the other. And here, where its breadth is least, it takes a month to cross it. 'Tis all composed of hills and valleys of sand, and not a thing to eat to be found on it. But after riding for a day and a night you find fresh water, enough mayhap for some 50 or 100 persons with their beasts, but not for more. And all across the Desert you will find water in like manner, that is to say, in some 28 places altogether you will find good water, but in no great quantity; and in four places you will find brackish water.

Beasts there are none, for there is nought for them to eat. But there is a marvellous thing related of this Desert, which is that when travellers are on the move by night, and one of them chances to lag behind or to fall asleep or the like, when he tries to gain his company again he will hear spirits talking, and will suppose them to be his comrades (*ode parlare spiriti in aria, che sembrano essere i suoi compagni*). Sometimes the spirits will call him by name; and thus shall a traveller ofttimes be led astray so that he never finds his party. And in this way many have perished.

Sometimes the stray travellers will hear as it were the tramp and hum of a great cavalcade of people away from the real line of the road; and taking this to be their own company they will follow the sound; and when the day breaks they will find that a cheat has been put on them and that they are in ill plight. Even in the daytime one hears these spirits talking. And sometimes you shall hear the sound of a variety of musical instruments, and still more commonly the sounds of drums. Hence in making this journey 'tis customary for travellers to keep close together. All the animals too have bells at their necks, so that they cannot easily get astray. And at sleeping time a signal is put up to show the direction of the next march.

So thus it is that the Desert is crossed.[1]

---

[1] The explanation of the 'voices' in the Desert of Lop is to be found in the account of an English explorer, Major Dalrymple Bruce, who in 1907 accomplished the overland journey from Simla to Peking.

He wrote a book about it, appropriately called *In the Footsteps of Marco Polo*.

The voices are heard in winter, which in those latitudes means the greater

Such a description must have interested the Venetians very little. What attraction could there be for them in wind-swept deserts, where the path was marked only by the skeletons of men and beasts who had fallen by the way? The curiosity of merchants was not roused by tales of hardship and of danger. The lure that proved a lode-star for them, was the unparalleled splendour of Kublai's Court. This is the sort of thing that made their mouths water:

> In a certain part of the hall where the Great Khan holds his table, there stands a great vessel of pure gold, holding as much as an ordinary butt; and at each corner of the great vessel is one of smaller size, of the capacity of a firkin, and from the former, the wine or beverage is drawn off into the latter. And on the buffet are set all the Lord's drinking vessels, among which are certain pitchers of the finest gold, which are called *verniques*, and are big enough to hold drink for eight or ten persons. And one of these is put between every two persons, besides a couple of golden cups with handles, so that every man helps himself from the pitcher that stands between him and his neighbour. And the ladies are supplied in the same way. The value of these pitchers and cups is something immense; in fact, the Great Khan has such a quantity of this kind of plate, and of gold and silver in other shapes, as no one before saw or heard of, or could believe.

or this:

> And on his birthday, the Great Khan dresses in the best of his robes, all wrought with beaten gold; and full 12,000 Barons and

part of the year. Along the borders of the marshes, such as those of Kara Koshun, when you camp for the night, you will hear the sounds of musical instruments and of drums. They are nothing else than the groaning and thunder of the floes, as the thermometer drops and the ice freezes harder.

Another subject of the Venetian Republic, the Blessed Odoric of Pordenone, spoke of a valley, where evil spirits dwelt in the rocks: 'And I heard therein sundry kinds of music, but chiefly nakers, which were marvellously played upon.' Such holy men as Fra Odorico and Friar Marchesino da Bassano, his companion, might recall verse 43 in the Twelfth Chapter of the Gospel according to St. Matthew: 'When the unclean spirit is gone out of man, he walketh through dry places, seeking rest.'

Knights on that day come forth dressed in robes of the same colour, and precisely like those of the Great Khan, except that they are not so costly; but still they are of the same colour, and are also of silk and gold. Every man so clothed has also a girdle of gold; and this as well as the dress is given him by the Sovereign. And I will aver that there are some of these suits decked with so many pearls and precious stones that a single suit shall be worth full 10,000 golden bezants.

*　　　*　　　*

Of the house—called the Ca' Polo—where the Polo family lived in Venice, near the church of San Grisostomo, only an old doorway remains in what is *la Corte del Milion*. The house itself was pulled down long ago. The doorway is interesting for it was there that the three Polos, Maffeo, Niccolò and Marco, returning from Cathay, knocked for admittance. A voice from inside asked the usual question:

'*Chi x'è?*'

Maffeo answered: '*El paròn!*' (The Master!)

But after more than twenty years of absence, the same fate awaited these wanderers as awaited Ulysses on his return to Ithaca. No one recognized them. Their relations, who had given them up for dead long ago, were reluctant to hand over their house and their possession to these three men of uncouth and outlandish appearance. They could hardly speak or understand the Venetian tongue and had acquired a likeness to the Tartar's, among whom they had lived. They were dressed in shabby coats of oriental cut, contrasting strangely with the rich raiment of gentlemen of the Ca' Polo. Then it was that the three travellers devised a scheme by which they should bring about their recognition. The story is one that is famous in Venetian history. It was first told by the Senator Gaspare Malipiero, and reported a century or more after the event, by Giambattista Ramusio:

MERCHANTS OF VENICE

They invited a number of their kindred to an entertainment, which they took care to have prepared with great state and splendour in that house of theirs; and when the hour arrived for sitting down at table they came forth of their chamber all three clothed in crimson satin, fashioned in long robes reaching to the ground, such as people in those days wore within doors. And when water for the hands had been served, and the guests were set, they took off those robes and put on others of crimson damask, whilst the first suits were by their orders cut up and divided among the servants. Then after partaking of some of the dishes they went out again and came back in robes of crimson velvet, and when they had taken their seats, the second suits were divided as before. When dinner was over they did the like with the robes of velvet, after they had put on dresses of the ordinary fashion worn by the rest of the company. These proceedings caused much wonder and familiarity among the guests when the cloth had been drawn and all the servants had been ordered to retire from the dining-hall. Messer Marco, as the youngest of the three, rose from table, and, going into another chamber, brought forth the three shabby dresses of coarse stuff which they had worn when they first arrived. Straightway they took sharp knives and began to rip up some of the seams and welts, and to take out of them jewels of the greatest value in vast quantities, such as rubies, sapphires, carbuncles, diamonds and emeralds, which had all been stitched up in those dresses in so artful a fashion that nobody could have suspected the fact. For when they took leave of the Great Khan, they had changed all the wealth he had bestowed upon them into this mass of rubies, emeralds and other jewels, being well aware of the impossibility of carrying with them so great an amount in gold over a journey of such extreme length and difficulty. Now this exhibition of such a huge treasure of jewels and precious stones, all tumbled out upon the table, threw the guests into fresh amazement, insomuch that they seemed quite bewildered and dumbfounded. And now they recognized that in spite of all former doubts these were in truth those honoured and worthy gentlemen of the Ca' Polo that they claimed to be; and so all paid them the greatest honour and reverence. And when the story got wind in Venice, straightway the whole city, gentle and simple, flocked to the house to embrace them, and to make much of them, with every conceivable demonstration of affection and of respect. On Messer Maffeo, who was the eldest, they conferred the honours of an office that was of great dignity in those days; whilst the young men came daily to visit and converse with the ever polite and gracious Messer Marco, and to ask him questions about Cathay and the Great Khan, all which he answered with such kindly courtesy that every man felt himself in a manner in his debt. And as it happened that in the story, which he was constantly called upon to repeat, of the magnificence of the Great Khan, he would speak of his revenues as amounting to ten or fifteen *millions* of gold; and in the like manner, when recounting other instances of great wealth in those parts, would always make use of the term *millions,* so they gave him the nickname of MESSER MARCO MILIONI, a thing which I have noted also in the Public Books of this Republic, where mention is made of him. The Court of his house also, at San Giovanni Chrisostomo, has always from that time been popularly known as the Court of the Milioni.

*   *   *

The travels and discoveries of Marco Polo, as recorded in his book, while they inspired Columbus with the idea of sailing to Cathay by way of the west, served the more immediate purpose of encouraging Venetian traders to extend their already opulent traffic beyond the Levant, with which they were already familiar, into the very heart of Asia. They carried their wares to the marts of Samarkand, crossing the lands then known as Tartary. From the shores of the Caspian they set sail to the mouth of the Volga and up that river as far as they could go; then overland once more to the Don, and then again in boats towards the north. . . . Since the days of the Phœnicians, the world had never known such dauntless traffickers. The prophet Isaiah might have spoken of Venice, as of Tyre

'. . . *the crowning city, whose merchants are princes, whose traffickers are the honourable of the earth*'.

They collected aromatic gums they sought for balm in Gilead. They turned the Crusades to their own uses, and made money out of the Holy Land, buying and selling relics, as if they were spices. Like England at a later date, they were not above trafficking in slaves.

Those were the days when robber barons were giving way to the courtly knights of chivalry. These proved excellent customers, buying for their ladies the gorgeous stuffs, precious stones and costly perfumes of the East.

It is in the natural order of things that such a genius as Shakespeare's should have seized upon such a theme, so that a merchant of Venice became immortal.

The reader may ask: do merchants of Venice still exist? Are any of them left? Certainly, as a national group, they are extinct. But individuals of that type, speaking the Venetian dialect, are still distributed between Venice, Padua and Trieste. You will find them in palatial offices, belonging to prosperous limited companies, and in the dingy rooms of tiny apartments in the *calli* around St. Mark's: less pretentious concerns, but not necessarily less successful, or with interests less widespread.

I have known one or two of them, such as Edgardo Morpurgo, for many years chairman of a big insurance company, and Giuseppe Volpi, Count of Misurata. But although they are dead and their place knows them no more, I cannot think of them as ghosts—I mean as something nebulous, outside this world of ours, condemned to disappear at cockcrow. I prefer to think of them as having been a first reincarnation of merchants of other days. Volpi, for example, might well have been the reincarnation of Marcantonio Barbaro, whose villa at Maser (near Asolo) he bought and restored for his daughter Marina. This is the same Marcantonio Barbaro, mentioned in this book, in the chapter dealing with Venetian diplomats. He was detained by the Turks in Constantinople, as a hostage during the war of Cyprus. There is a portrait of him that might justify my idea of his being reincarnated in Volpi. There was a certain physical resemblance between them. And they both possessed a characteristic Venetian taste for magnificence.

In Venice, magnificence was not the dull ceremonial and *punctilio* of Spain, nor the mere dazzle of costume, such as the Magyars took pride in. It was based on a sense of beauty, and developed in the Venetians much as a genius for music developed in other races. It expressed itself in a pageantry that became more and more splendid as wealth increased.

One might compare it to a genius for stage-management. That Volpi possessed this genius was proved when, together with Rheinhardt, he organized an open-air performance of the *Merchant of Venice* on the Campo San Trovaso. A real bridge formed part of the scenery and was used by the actors, giving an effect of realism that enhanced the loveliness of the performance.

Edgardo Morpurgo was a 'merchant' of another type. The Lion of St. Mark's did not always appear in his dealings, but was there incognito. I realized, when in China, how vast were the interests he controlled, extending into the Pacific, including the Philippines.

His principal centre was in Trieste, and I remember his coming away from there, in the spring of 1915, when it became clear that we would soon be at war with Austria. This meant abandoning 'for the duration' vast interests on the eastern shores of the Adriatic and the Balkans, not to mention the various provinces of the Hapsburg Empire. Small losses might seem not worth bothering about in comparison, but—of course—a true merchant does not reason like that. Morpurgo was not going to give even small things away.

He turned up in Venice, carrying a little black bag that appeared strangely heavy for its size. It was full of gold. Not much to salvage from such a wreck, but better than nothing. He did not return empty-handed to Rialto.

10

THE DIPLOMATS

> It was a beautiful thing that these two Princes [*Francis I, King of France, and Charles V, Roman Emperor and King of Spain*] who were such great enemies, and waged war against each other with so much hatred, never ceased, during this time, to negotiate, by various means, with the object of reaching an agreement and concluding peace. Which thing was very well done, not only because those efforts were ultimately crowned with success, but because it showed great wisdom. One should never face so determinedly in one direction, as not to be able to keep an eye on the other.
>
> Report of MARINO CAVALLI,
> *Venetian Ambassador to the Court of France*

IN the estimation of their contemporaries, no diplomats stood higher than those of Venice. Foreigners of distinction—even foreign kings—came from afar to study their methods.

When a Venetian ambassador had concluded a mission abroad, he would make a final report, or *Relazione,* a comprehensive summing up of his judgments and activities, and he would read it aloud to the Doge and Senate. It would be difficult to present history in a more animated and vigorous form.[1]

[1] Various collections have been made and published, at one time or another, of these *Relazioni.*

The best known and the most complete is the collection edited by Signor Eugenio Albèri, and published in Florence in the year 1863, thanks to the munificence of the Marchese Gino Capponi and others, who provided the requisite funds. There are about twenty volumes, which represent, in a sense, a continuation of the diaries of Marin Sanudo and of the Altino Chronicle. These form the basis of early Venetian history.

Some of these reports cover periods of several years, such as Pietro Duodo's *Relazione al Senato*, concerning a mission to France, which began when Henry IV of Navarre entered Paris as King of France, after his conversion to catholicism (*'Paris vaut bien une messe'!*). It describes events during the next five years, and was so long that it took the author two days to read it to the Senate (12th and 13th January 1598).

Other *Relazioni* are merely the account of a brief ceremonial visit and give us glimpses of a foreign capital on some special occasion; they are like snap-shots of history. One of these is a report by Giovanni Cappello, after his mission to Vienna, to congratulate the Emperor Ferdinand on his accession (A.D. 1558), on the abdication of Charles V. This ambassador remained in what then called itself the capital of 'The Holy Roman Empire' during three months. He describes the Viennese as hastening the defences of their city. The Turks were then no further off than Buda, almost within sight of the watchers on the Stephans Dom, the high steeple of the cathedral. Houses were being hurriedly demolished to build the defences that enclosed the *Innere Stadt*, and where now is the famous avenue called the Ring.

When the weak Latin Empire of Byzantium was submerged by what Carlyle called 'the unspeakable Turk', the Ottoman Empire came to represent the principal danger for Venice. The reports from the ambassadors to the Sultan in Constantinople are among the lengthiest and the most detailed. But not all the *Relazioni* contain information collected and transmitted in a normal diplomatic capacity. Marcantonio Barbaro was Venetian ambassador in Constantinople when war broke out (over Cyprus) between Turkey and Venice. The Turks, violating the sanctity of an envoy, detained him as a hostage. He seems, however, to have been able to send some news home, and was released after five years. His *Relazione*, made to the Doge and Senate after he got back, relates what he had seen and heard during his detention. He tells—for example—how one

Pasha was all for peace, fearing that his rivals would accumulate too much wealth and gain too much power, continuing hostilities, not for the good of the State, but to further their own interests.

In those days, every educated Venetian, when abroad, was encouraged to collect information and to make reports concerning what he had occasion to observe in foreign parts. Thus, in Elizabethan times, Venetian clerks, employed in the export of their national goods to London, would write home from England, giving their impressions. Most of them complained that it was impossible to get the English to work or do any business between Friday evening and Monday morning. Their love of the countryside took them out of town for a long week-end! *Nihil sub sole novum!*

A report by Vincenzo Querini, after a mission to Lisbon, in 1506, is of exceptional interest. The author had gone to Lisbon from Spain, after the death of Isabella 'the Catholic', Queen of Castile. He writes about the possible outcome of recent journeys by Portuguese navigators. The discovery of an all-sea route to the Far East, round the Cape of Good Hope, represented a formidable threat to the monopoly enjoyed up till then by Venice in providing Europe with eastern products and spices. Here we have the fear of changing conditions, born in a far-seeing diplomat, who forewarned his government of an inevitable decline in the fortunes of the City.

Giovanni Sagredo, in the year 1654, gives the Venetian Senate a portrait of Oliver Cromwell, in which it is not easy to recognize the dour, unswerving puritanical soldier:

He is a man of fifty-six years, with a scanty beard, loose-fitting clothes, small, robust and of martial bearing.

His ways are dark and deep; he carries a long sword at his side. It is not possible to know what religious rite he favours; guided by the interest of the State, he changes his religion. This is not difficult, for he says himself there are 246 religions professed in London—and this is a weakness, advantageous to his policy. It is impossible to deny that his glory has come to him through his genius and activities; he is certainly brave, ingenious and prudent, but one must admit that he has been a favourite of fortune; he is a man of the sword and tongue, and in order better to persuade, he often has recourse to tears, weeping more for other people's sins than for his own.[1]

Two hundred and forty-six religions, less than a century after the Reformation, seems a good deal. Voltaire only put them at 100.

What else do we find in the Venetian archives? What are the subjects under consideration? We hear of the struggle for world-dominion between those two *colossi*, France and Spain, with England hovering in the background and trying to keep the balance of power. We read of formidable pressure exerted on the Western states by a bellicose and expansive East. We hear of the break-up of Christian unity after the Reformation. Meanwhile—though the *Relazioni* do not say so—in art, literature and science, the Renaissance renews the forward march of human progress, after the long pause of the Middle Ages.

In the midst of so much wisdom and so much strength, the historian becomes aware of one weak point, common to all the states into which the Italian peninsula is divided: their inability to come to a reasonable understanding with political and commercial rivals. Italians failed to achieve national unity, even in the form of a confederation. They looked back nostalgically to the greatness that had been theirs under Rome,

[1] The following is the Italian text:

E' uomo di 56 anni, con una barba rada, un abito largo, piccolo, robusto, marziale in apparenza. Il suo contegno è oscuro e profondo, porta al fianco una grande spada. Non è possibile sapere quale rito religioso egli segua: guidato dagli interessi dello Stato, egli cambia religione, ciò che non è difficile, dicendo egli stesso che a Londra se ne professano 246, ciò che li indebolisce e s'accorda con la sua politica. E' impossibile negare che dal suo genio e dalla sua attività non sia derivata la sua gloria: certo egli è coraggioso, ingegnoso e prudente, ma conviene riconoscere che fu un favorito della fortuna; è uomo di spada e lingua, e per essere più persuasivo si vale spesso delle lacrime, piangendo più per i peccati degli altri che per i propri.

and learnt by bitter experience that the coherence of one nation, achieved at any cost, would have been better than a divided weakness in face of foreign armies.

Venetian arms set up the winged lion in many a market place along the Adriatic coast, as a warning to other maritime powers to keep off. Those were years of an unremitting inter-urban warfare, in which Venice was the rival, not only of Genoa, but of Pisa. On the mainland, Pavia rivalled Ravenna, Siena fought with Florence, Gubbio with Perugia. Guelph was against Ghibelline, Montacute against Capulet, and so forth and so on *ad infinitum*. But it is also true that the green countryside, in many a pleasant land beside Italy, served as a battlefield for never-ending Wars of the Roses.

*   *   *

It is only natural that I, who have Venetian blood in my veins, should have a feeling of admiration and respect for those diplomats of other days, who could sign themselves with the proud qualification *Divi Marci Procurator*! I did once sign a treaty as the plenipotentiary of my King, but never as attorney for one of the twelve apostles!

Some time ago, I wrote a 'Handbook of the Perfect Diplomat' (extracts from which can be found in two of my publications).[1] A similar manual was written in the sixteenth century by a Venetian diplomat, Marino Cavalli, after he had been ambassador at the court of Charles V, in 1543 in France in 1560, in Rome in 1566 and in Constantinople during the following years. Like Lord Chesterfield, he condensed his knowledge for the instruction of his son. This was Sigismund, who was ambassador in Bavaria, in 1565, and later at the court of the Duke of Savoy.

Thus it happens that we have two different sources of information concerning Marino: his *Relazioni* to the Senate

[1] *Laughing Diplomat* and *The Two Impostors* (John Murray—1938 and 1949).

and the handbook called *Informatione dell'Offitio dell'Ambasciatore.*

This treatise is inevitably a little out of date.

Nowadays, an ambassador need not give advice as to the care of his armour, or the length of his sword (which should not be too long, or it will get muddy in bad weather). Nor need he carry tents about with him, for travel in countries, such as Hungary and Turkey, where accommodation left much to be desired.

The author says that the tents should not be too big and pretentious, lest the wind carry them off, as once occurred to the Marquis Joachim of Brandenburg (A.D. 1542), whose tent was swept away in a storm, leaving the inmates under the rain, so that they had to take refuge where Marino Cavalli and his suite were lodged.

The handbook goes into the matter of tents with much detail, for it often happened, in those days, that an ambassador had to follow the army commanded by the monarch to whom he was accredited. Practical advice is given about bedding and sanitation, a matter almost more important (if possible) then than it is now, for fear of the plague still haunted the most cheerful and sanguine diplomats.

We should hold in great esteem this duty of maintaining the health of the gentlemen and servants who accompany the Ambassador. Even when all commodities and remedies are at hand, if one is ill, he creates disturbance for all those in the family who are well. Think what this means in the household of an Ambassador, when he is on the move, in localities where there are no doctors, nor apothecaries, nor any one who could bleed the patient (*trar sangue*), as once happened to me in the village of Troly in Picardy. Besides which, we should also take all possible precautions for the welfare and the health of the retainers, who should be dear to us as if they were our own children. We should look ahead, to make sure, as much as possible, that they do not suffer. . . . When one of them falls ill, it often happens that they all do at the same time. When this happens, the Ambassador will be the most unhappy creature in the world; and more so, if he finds himself in the necessity of leaving one behind, who has died, or is sick unto death. Much have I learnt of these things, when I was in sore straits, following the armies in France and in Hungary. . . .

With a practical mind, such as he possessed, and travelling as much as he did, Cavalli acquired much experience in judging horseflesh. He advises that an ambassador's stable should not be organized so much in view of making a good show, as with the object of providing reliable means of transport. He points out that it would be unwise to buy twelve beautiful Arabs at the cost of 1,200 *scudi* each, if the hardships of travel were to put them all out of action. This might well occur if they are not sturdy animals, well used to rough going and to the frequent misfortunes of the road. If one has horses of too delicate a breed, it is more than likely that the whole mission will find itself, sooner or later, reduced to travelling on foot, 'a contingency which, for an Ambassador is both uncomfortable and undignified'.

When speaking of the staff of an embassy, Marino Cavalli called it *familia*. It is clear that he really did consider it as being *pro tem* on a par with his own family. He had fewer collaborators than a modern *Chef de Mission*, one gentleman in waiting, one secretary and one page. It is quite clear that Marino's secretary must have had a lot to do, even though there must have been much less clerical work than in our modern chanceries. The handbook recommends that he should not claim too many privileges, so as to get himself disliked by the rest of the staff, and insists that, if he had a servant of his own, this servant should not know how to read and write, lest he learn too much of confidential negotiations.

It is odd to find a farrier among the members of a diplomatic mission, and a *credenziero*, or 'cupboard man', whose duties comprised that of travelling ahead of the ambassador, in order to prepare accommodation for him and his suite. The *credenziero* would be doubly useful if he could act as a barber and hair-dresser, just as it was advisable that the chief stableman should be also a cobbler, to mend, if not to make, boots and shoes.

All this sounds very far away from 'the whirl of royalty and diplomatic splendour', that figures to-day in the cheaper forms of transatlantic literature. But the material side of diplomatic life—as I well know—may include emergencies, such as milking a cow and blacking one's own boots, besides (for the ladies) making their own clothes!

In his handbook, Marino speaks with sober good sense of the various duties, assigned to members of his *familia*. But he becomes almost lyrical when he comes to the cook!

I had one in France, who was called William the Norman. His pay was V *scudi* a month. It was a real pleasure to have such a one, and he gave me much contentment of the soul (*estrema contenteza d'animo*). In a very short time, he would prepare a dinner, with so much precision and good judgment, that all kinds of viands would be ready as soon as required. And when he had finished his work in the kitchen, he would appear at table with the fruit, always neat and well groomed, with a gold chain round his neck, and he would like to hear what the guests had to say about the courses that had been served and about those still on the table, being much pleased when they were praised; and if ever somebody said the contrary, he did not answer, but after they had left, it was admirable to hear him defend himself and denounce those who had reprehended him . . .

. . . I gave a banquet in Nuremberg to the Elector Palatine, the Duke William of Bavaria, the Cardinal of Trent, the Bishops of Eichstadt and Würzburg, and Count Frederick of Fürstenberg, all people of the highest standing in the country. My cook served us fifteen courses, all in different colours, and with the fruit he gave gloves, shoes, hams, and brooches, all of sugar and almonds, beautiful to see and delightful to taste. Finally the fame of this man at Court became so great, that from my kitchen he passed to that of the Emperor Charles V, as second cook, with a pay of XV *scudi* a month.

The best thing that an Ambassador can have in his house is a good cook, for in a forest, with one calf, he can prepare a dinner of X courses. With every herb and every fruit he will make sauces and condiments, and other delicacies most pleasant and enjoyable. I remember once, in Vienna, having an Italian cook, who made excellent torte and ravioli, such as they have in Lombardy. The Bishop of Erlau, who was a Frangipani, begged me to send him a large plate of ravioli, for he never thought of Lombardy without having a wish to eat ravioli. Frangipani was beautifully served with two plates, and he did me the honour to send one of the two as a gift to the King (who is now the Emperor Ferdinand), telling him whence it came, so that there was much talk for some time about this dish. Which things bring much grace to an Ambassador in any Court.

*　　　*　　　*

The fall of Byzantium had substituted a hostile for a friendly state on the shores of the Bosphorus. At the time, Marino Cavalli disapproved of some of the instructions sent to the Venetian Ambassador at Constantinople, telling him to assure the Sultan of the unchanging friendship of Venice. Similar assurances—he maintained—should only be given 'conditionally'.

We should proceed with ability somewhere between the two courses: to make war, or not to make it. Most certainly we should not go to war, but we must not let them think that this is because we cannot do so. . . . We should keep them suspended, as long as possible, between hope and fear.

The danger to Venice was not only a military one, nor entirely due to the closing of markets to expand in. It was an economic danger in another sense. For some time, Venice still continued to import grain from her lost colonies that had become Ottoman possessions. This was for the maintenance of the inhabitants and garrisons on Levantine islands, and even for re-victualling her fleets. Marino Cavalli perceived the danger of the situation, and pointed it out in forcible language:

Let us face the truth! What forces are ours, with such a dearth of food? Of what use are our armies, without bread? What are our peoples, if they have to beg for alms at our doors? They can be left to starve by our friends no less than our enemies, or kept in such straits that they cannot move! What dignity is that of a State that goes begging for bread, from christians and from infidels? Living always on the goodwill of others and impoverishing our Treasury of the bullion that—God forbid!—may be lacking under the stress of war?

The remedies are not easy, but they are necessary. Otherwise, in a short time, we will come to the end of our resources, and find ourselves unable to endure our deficiencies, or to repair them. Hunger has done great things in the world; let us keep these things in mind, night and day, taking every possible precaution. This is a graver issue even than war. Reputation is of great importance to a Prince, but what will ours be if we cannot nourish our peoples without charity? Let us acquire more territory, or diminish the useless mouths, or let us cultivate the country so that we can feed them all. The high cost of grain is all to my personal advantage. But here I am not speaking as a private person, but as a public official. And even in my private capacity, I can look ahead, and realize that I also would suffer from a public calamity.

*   *   *

The character and the qualities of a reigning monarch, being all-important in those days, it was useful that an ambassador should be good at direct portraiture. Like Titian, Cavalli has left us portraits (word portraits this time) of Charles V, Francis I and Suleiman the Magnificent.

This is what he writes about the Emperor:

He uses all diligence to understand every detail of the matters that concern him, and not a *scudo* is spent in his household but what he sees the receipt. . . . He is very dilatory in remunerating his servants, and this is intentional, for thus he obliges them to continue, if they do not wish to lose their money and their jobs. When he pays them—which he does one time only—he gives most generously, thus raising hopes in the others and encouraging the beneficiaries to put up with further labours. It is his will that they take what he gives, or leave his service. . . .

He always speaks humanely; never shows anger, never boasts, but always has in his words that which is just and hope in God. His speech is always based on reason, so that you might think of him that he has never said anything deserving of blame, or anything that brought harm to himself or to what is his. He never gives an answer without first consulting the Signor de Granvelle. During negotiations he can use—when convenient—expressions that are very ambiguous, so that it behoves ambassadors to be careful. . . . He is stern on points of honour as over all the smaller matters that figure in contracts of peace and in the alliances that he stipulates with others. He pardons offences to himself and to his people, when it suits him to do so. He is firmly fixed in his opinions and never appears to do anything because he is forced to. He will let the world go to ruin, rather than submit to violence. He makes great account of princes or private persons, who could serve him or harm him, but this is not apparent in his manner or in his reputation. He is not bloodthirsty or revengeful, seeking the total ruin of his enemies; he seeks to weaken them, not to destroy. Rarely does he punish a dependant, even putting up with more than he should, and he is a valiant supporter of his representatives even in actions taken against his own orders. He is very well informed, if in great secrecy, from all sides; he will sit in a chair, talking matters over four or five hours at a time, and sometimes he will set down in writing the pros and cons, in order to decide which appears to be the better way. Sometimes he will keep a courier waiting for days on end, to think over in cold blood, whether decisions taken still seem to him good. . . . He will keep negotiations waiting in the hopes of a favourable opportunity to obtain what he wants, and sometimes it happens to him to do so after twenty-five or thirty years. . . .

Marino Cavalli took no pay for his eleven years' service. When they were over, and he had defrayed the expenses out of his own purse, he asked only that he might be allowed to keep the gold chain that he had been given by Charles V.

In support of this modest request, he reminded the Doge and the Senate that his missions abroad had cost him enough to have given a rich dowry to his beloved daughter Contarina, and that, in going from one place to another he had ridden, in all, some 18,000 miles. His estates near Verona, so he affirmed, were nearly ruined by the fact that they had been long administered by women and children.

I have quoted at some length from Marino's writings, and I would conclude by recalling his last will and testament, a lengthy document, carefully drafted. In it he advises his descendants to hold together and to love one another. 'If this be not possible, put up with one another.'

And he adds that they should not consider themselves as Princes and Dukes. Their greatest pride should be to be known as Venetian gentlemen, faithful servants of the Republic.

Here is an aristocrat at its best.

II

GHOSTS OF LEPANTO

Immortal waves that saw Lepanto's fight
BYRON—*Childe Harold's Pilgrimage*—Canto IV

AT seven o'clock in the evening of the 7th October 1571, Pope Pius V (Michele Ghislieri) was going over accounts with his Treasurer, Brunoti. The Pope was weakened by illness and prolonged fasts and the work tired him, so that he often sighed with weariness. His emaciated face had a double tuft of beard at the end of his chin, and when reading the figures, he tilted his head a little to one side, much as a bird does, when looking at something near-by.

Of a sudden, he stopped and got up from the table, going to the window, which he opened. He stood there for some time, gazing out into the distance. The window faced eastward. After a while, he turned back into the room, and then the Treasurer noticed that all the weariness in the Pope's face had left it. His expression was radiant.

'No more work to-day,' he said. 'The Christian fleet has gained a great victory over the Turks. We must go and thank God for all His mercies. . . .'

When he went out of the Presence, the Treasurer rather imprudently told what had happened while he was with the Pope, and in consequence great expectations were raised in the Vatican.

But as time passed—five days, ten days, a fortnight—and no news arrived to confirm the Pope's vision, people lost heart and murmured that the Holy Father was old and sick, and had hallucinations. Pius himself was racked with anxiety. During the past years he had striven to bring some unity among the Christian forces in Europe (appealing even to the Swiss Cantons and to the German protestants), hoping to persuade them to form a League for their common defence against Mahommedan aggression. Cyprus had been wrested from the Venetians, Malta had only been saved at the last moment, after a heroic resistance under the leadership of La Vallette.

One cannot say that the fall of Cyprus sent a sudden thrill of fear through all Europe, for in those days news travelled slowly. But when it came, first to one country and then to another, it provoked a feeling of such horror against the Turks, that the imagination of the Western nations was stirred, and the echo of that horror reverberated throughout the centuries, and was heard again in Mr. Gladstone's voice, condemning the 'Bulgarian' and the 'Armenian' atrocities, also in Carducci's poem, *La Mietitura del Turco*.

> *Il Turco miete. Eran le teste armene*
> *Che ier cadean sotto il ricurvo acciar:*
> *Ei le offriva boccheggianti e oscene*
> *A i pianti de l'Europa a imbalsamar.*

The Sultan Selim II, who succeeded to Suleiman the Magnificent, was nicknamed 'the toper'. It was said of him that he wished to conquer Cyprus, not so much for its copper mines, as for the excellent wine produced on the island. In 1570, he landed an army of 60,000 men. The capital, Nicosìa, defended by Niccolò Dandolo, was taken after forty-five days, and 20,000 of its inhabitants were put to the sword. The port of Famagusta, defended by Marcantonio Bragadino, made a protracted resistance of nearly a year. It had to capitulate, in August 1571, owing to lack of food and of munitions. The terms of the capitulation were shamefully violated by the Turks, who put the Commander to death with cruel torments.

In his admirable book on Venetian History, William Roscoe Thayer (Macmillan, New York 1905) describes the events:

> Marcantonio Bragadino learnt of the fall of Nicosìa when Niccolò Dandolo's head was thrown into his lines by the Turks.
>
> To him, the Turks offered what appeared to be reasonable terms. On the agonized entreaties of his people, food and powder having given out, he capitulated on August the 18th. But Mustapha gave up the city to the sack. He caused Lorenzo Tiepolo to be gibbeted. Baglioni, Martinengo and Querini were hewn to pieces in his presence. Happy they, compared with the gallant Barbarigo, who was first mutilated, then hoisted to the yardarm of the tallest galley, so that the Turks might deride him and the captive Venetians be terrorized. After eleven days of unremitting tortures, the brave Bragadino, whose courage never flinched, was flayed alive. He died dauntlessly, reciting the Miserere and calling to Christ to support him. His skin was stuffed with straw, and after Mustapha's minions had heaped indignities on it to satiety, it was hung at a peak of a Turkish vessel, which carried it in triumph to Constantinople.

Though the Spaniards considered Venice as an obstacle to their hegemony on the mainland of Italy and elsewhere, these grim events on the Mediterranean alarmed them into an ephemeral activity, incited, as they were, by the Pope.

On 7th October, less than two months after the fall of Cyprus, the united fleets of the Christian powers, after many failures, did actually face the fleet which flew the Crescent flag. The agreement among those Christian powers was sadly belated, for, during the reign of Suleiman the Magnificent, the victorious Crescent had been hoisted over Belgrade, Budapest, Temesvar, Rhodes, Tabriz, Baghdad, Aden and Algiers.

The Pope's intuition had been right, when he gazed out over the roofs of Rome, and declared a victorious battle was drawing to its close. It was indeed one of the great naval battles of the world, like that of Actium and of Trafalgar. It was also the last big naval battle ever to be fought between vessels manned with oars.

The general command of the Christian fleet had been assigned to young (he was only twenty-six years old) Don John of Austria, an illegitimate son of the late Emperor Charles V, and therefore a natural brother of King Philip II, who however was jealous of him and refused to concede to him the title of Infante of Spain. The fleet of the League consisted of 200 galleys and eight galleasses, the bulk of which came from Venice. The Spaniards sent only 24 ships. Other contingents were those of Genoa, under Gianandrea Doria; a papal contingent, under Marcantonio Colonna, and a squadron of the Knights of Malta.

The Turkish fleet had come up from Cyprus and Crete, full of that swaggering confidence that the French call *jactance*. Of the two opposing fleets, theirs had the greater numbers: 273 galleys, of a lighter build than those of the Christians. They emerged to do battle from the Gulf of Patras, on the West coast of Greece. The commander was Ali-Mouezzin Pasha, and his subordinates were Chulouk Bey, of Alexandria (known as 'Scirocco') and a renegade Italian, Uluk Ali, from Algiers.

The Christian fleet was formed in the traditional order of those days—a long line abreast, subdivided into a centre or 'battle', commanded by Don John in person; the left-wing under Barbarigo, and the right under Doria.

The Turks had the initial advantage. Ali Pasha's greater numbers enabled him to outflank the enemy, and his lighter ships charged in between the heavy galleasses and then turned to attack them. Only the better build of the Venetian ships, splendid seamanship and an admirable discipline gave the galleys commanded by Barbarigo the ultimate victory on the left-wing, though their commander lost his life.

In the centre, Don John fought with consummate skill and

great dash and bravery. But a false move of Doria's on the right-wing imperilled the whole Christian fleet.

Muskets and artillery were used on both sides, but the Turks still relied on bows and arrows. It was an arrow that struck Barbarigo in the eye, depriving him of speech for three days, before he died. Don John himself was slightly wounded by an arrow, and found himself in great danger, when two Venetian captains, Loredano and Malipiero, plunged into the fight around him, diverting the peril from their chief, at the cost of their own lives. Don John then renewed the combat with his principal antagonist, Ali Pasha, grappling with and boarding his galley. Ali fell by a musket shot and then his crew laid down their arms. The Turkish commander's head was severed from his body and mounted on the top of a mast. In his book, *Essai sur les Moeurs*, Voltaire observes: '*C'était abuser du droit de guerre, mais ceux qui avaient écorché Bragadino, dans Famagouste, ne méritaient pas un autre traitement*'.

Still, the fate of Christendom hung in the balance, when John of Austria decided, almost as a last resource, to liberate the rowers, chained to the oars below-decks, and to give them arms. These men flung themselves into the fray, boarding the Turkish ships, side by side with the proud hidalgos of Spain. The Turks, to avoid being overwhelmed, liberated their own galley-slaves. But they were mostly Christian prisoners, with years of ill-treatment to avenge. They turned on their Moslem captors and fought on the side of the League.

But how was it that the news of this victory delayed so long in reaching Rome? Don John did not fail to send a messenger to the Pope, asking him to convey the joyful news to all the monarchs in Christendom, whose forces had served the common cause. But storms and contrary winds prevented the arrival of the messenger (the Venetian, Contarini). Meanwhile, Sebastiano Venier, who had succeeded Barbarigo, well knowing that the Senate would expect to be informed directly, sent a messenger of his own, Giustiniani, to Venice, unbeknown to Don John, who afterwards showed bitter resentment.

The Pope was woken up in the night, sixteen days after the battle, by a messenger from Venice, congratulating the Holy Father, and thus confirming his vision of the seventh October evening. The Pope had everyone roused in the Vatican, to join him in a thanksgiving service. To the victorious Don John of Austria, he sent a message, quoting the sixth verse of the first chapter of the Gospel according to St. John: *Fuit homo missus a Deo, cui nomen erat Johannes.*

Though, as King of Sicily and Naples, Philip II had a major interest in warding off the Moslem danger, the joyful news was received by him in glacial silence. He was attending vespers in his chapel, when a messenger drew near and whispered in his ear. The courtiers around the King waited breathlessly for some sign of delight and pride. But Philip gave it not. He remained silent and indifferent. Never was his resentment more apparent at Don John's successes and popularity.

*　　*　　*

The advantages gained in the battle of Lepanto were squandered during the subsequent period of inaction, when, in the aftermath of victory, the rancour, the disagreements and the quarrelling between Allies, began again worse than ever.

It was Sebastiano Veniero who took this most to heart: the fierce, white-bearded old sea-captain who had taken the place of Barbarigo. He perceived the opportunity of destroying the Turkish menace, once and for all, and he felt that, as long as Venice was the back-bone of the League, the minor contingents should follow her lead. As they did not do so, and showed scant goodwill in the common enterprise, old Veniero could keep his temper with his fellow commanders only when they were actually fighting side by side under fire, boarding enemy ships and repulsing Turkish attempts to do the same. He was most happy when striking hard, with all the true warrior's zest at feeling his blows go home.

When the battle of Lepanto was over Veniero, bleeding and limping from a wound, went to present himself to John of Austria. The latter ran to him and embraced him, saying that the battle had shown what the Venetians could dare and do. But it was an ephemeral cordiality. And soon after the old man asked the Senate that someone 'more prudent' than himself should be given the command, lest, in his anger at the dilatory conduct of the campaign, he should say or do something that might bring prejudice to the interests of the Republic. He was replaced by Foscarini and came home. But soon after on the death of Doge Luigi Mocenigo, he was elected to succeed him, as head of the State.

*   *   *

In the church of San Giovanni e Paolo, in Venice, a tablet recalls the heroism of Bragadino, and a bronze statue shows Sebastiano Veniero, standing on the deck of his galley. According to his own wish, he was buried in the church of Santa Maria degli Angeli at Murano. But this church, during the nineteenth century, fell into decay and was not restored.

It was during my own boyhood that the question arose, whether so great a Venetian could be left to lie in an abandoned grave. And it was decided to bring his remains to Venice, to be interred in San Giovanni e Paolo, where the Venieros had a private chapel.

This was done in 1896, when the Syndic was Count Grimani. The cost of the removal amounted to 9,000 lire, which were then the equivalent of 180 dollars.

Old Sebastiano was known to have been a parsimonious person, who spent very little on himself. He once remarked that his house in Santa Maria Formosa was in such a state of disrepair that he could get nobody to rent it from him. It is

probable that he would have raised objections to the removal
of his bones, from one place to another, at so considerable an
expense!

*   *   *

The ghosts of Lepanto could be counted by tens of thousands,
yet they are but a small percentage of the innumerable phan-
toms who, in their day, took part in that endless drama, the
struggle, between East and West. It began, as far as we know,
between Greece and Persia, and then passed on to Rome and
Carthage, through the Crusades, to the wars against the
Saracens in the Mediterranean and the Moors in Spain. The
curtain has not fallen, even to-day, on the last act of that great
drama.

In the Middle Ages, Europe had to fight for survival against
both Mongol and Islamic invaders. The battles of Chalons,
Tours and Liegnitz, marked the culminating points in the
defence of the West against the Huns, the Arabs and the
Mongols. When (A.D. 770) the horn of Roland echoed in
the Pass of Roncesvalles, Asia began in Spain and on the right
bank of the Elbe.

The coloured races began to recede, like an outgoing tide,
about the time when Columbus discovered America. But the
fear of the Moslem was ever present, and Venice faced a danger
out of all proportion to her strength. The task of repelling
the Turk should have been shared by all Christendom. But
how could the Christian powers stand united, when hatred of
the Papist for Protestant and of Protestant for Papist far
exceeded the hatred of either for the Mahommedans?

In 1572, a year after Lepanto, the French Catholics were
massacring the Huguenots on the night of St. Bartholomew,
and the Spanish Catholics were striving to exterminate the
Protestants in Holland!

12

THE ADVENTURER

There is a misunderstanding that permeates all that is said
for or against the reality of spectral phenomena: i.e. spectral
phenomena present themselves entirely like bodily phenomena; but they are not such, and are not supposed to be
such. This distinction is difficult, and requires knowledge
of the matter, and even of philosophy and physiology.

For it is needful to comprehend that an influence like
that of a body does not necessarily involve the presence of
that body.

SCHOPENHAUER—Essay on Visions in *Parerga
und Paralipomena* (Berlin—1851)

THERE are few pleasanter sights than a young and pretty girl,
crouching on the stone flags of the Piazza, or sitting on the base
of one of the three tall flagstaffs, surrounded by an eager, fluttering crowd of pigeons, their plumage shot grey and purple, pecking
at the golden grains of Indian corn, held in the girl's open palm.

Late one afternoon in autumn, when gathering shadows
were soon to send the pigeons to roost among domes and
pinnacles and overhanging eaves, a very pretty girl was following the inevitable routine of feeding the *colombi*. She had
detached herself from a group of American tourists of a more
advanced age, sitting at the little round tables opposite
Florian's and partaking of ices and *paste*, which one of their
number alluded to as 'cookies'.

From out of one of the little Settecento rooms, with their
faded gold and tarnished looking-glasses, there emerged on the
open portico of the Procuratie Nuove a very tall, but shadowy
figure of a man wearing rather peculiar clothes. Fortunately

(for he would not have liked to be much noticed by the crowd), the raiment worn in Venice by foreign and native tourists is so varied, that peculiarities of dress attract little attention. This gentleman wore his hair very long and tied in a queue with a black ribbon, and he had lace ruffles at his throat and wrists. He cast a masterful, but uninterested, glance at the group of elderly ladies distributed round the café tables, and then his eye fell on the lovely figure further off: the girl feeding the pigeons. Without a moment's hesitation, he started off in her direction.

Catching sight of black silk breeches and of shoes with silver buckles and high red heels, the girl looked up to meet the admiring glance of a pair of roguish, laughing eyes, set in a face so dark and swarthy that it might have been that of an Arab.

'Hullo!' she exclaimed. 'And where do *you* come from?'

'From the infernal regions.'

She smiled, unbelieving. 'And what is it like there?'

'Not so bad. Plenty of good-looking women, though few of them as young as you are.'

'Can you come out, when you like?'

'Once a year, and then only till midnight. Not to waste time, I make straight for the Piazza. Since the first pigeons flew here, following the ship that bore the body of St. Mark, there's always been some attractive young lady anxious to feed them.'

The girl threw her last grains of corn to the birds and stood up dusting her hands. 'Say! You're a queer guy. Do you belong here?'

'I used to, till they put me in prison. I had to avoid the place for a while, after that.'

'After they let you out?'

'No. After I escaped.'

'You must come and tell the others about that. They'll be thrilled. And what is your name?'

'Giacomo Casanova, at your service.'

'You don't say so! Why, only yesterday, I saw you in a film.'

'You saw me in what?'

'In the *Adventures of Giacomo Casanova*. But it was in Italian, and I could not understand what was said.'

'And I was there?'

'Of course you were. . . . But the actor who took your part didn't look like you at all. He was very . . .'

The girl hesitated, and her companion finished the sentence for her.

'Very good-looking, which I am not. Is that so?'

'Well . . . perhaps. You're not offended?'

He laughed: 'Why should I be? It's only what Charles de Ligne used to say about me.'

'And what was that?'

'Only that I might have been a very handsome man, if I hadn't been ugly.'

'Well, anyway, you're twice the size of the actor in the film, and much more amusing. But you must come and be introduced to my family. Aunt Sadie has just bought a very expensive camera. She'll want to take some candid shots of you, to show to folk in Los Angeles.'

She took his consent for granted and started off, leading the way towards the group of elderly Americans at Florian's.

But when she turned to speak to him again, thinking that he was following her, Giacomo Casanova had vanished.

* * *

This little ghost story, or fantasy, was conceived after I had passed an hour or more in the old library, called La Marciana, which you enter through a doorway facing the Piazzetta and flanked by two huge male caryatides.

Rosolino Gattinoni, the librarian, was no relation of mine, though he may have been related to the Ruffini's (it was in my cousin Nane's house that I first met him). He was happy in a profession that put him in charge of the wonderful collection of books, of which the first nucleus was bequeathed to the *Serenissima* by Petrarch.

Rosolino and I had been browsing among the writings of Giacomo Casanova, culminating in the Memoirs that— published after his death—made him better known among the general public than many of his respectable contemporaries: for example, than Izaak Newton or Gottfried Leibnitz.

I left Rosolino among his treasures (he seemed to consider them his own) and walked across to the 'Unione'. The windows of this Club look out on the Piazza from the corner above the Mercerie, next to the clock-tower with the bronze bell-ringers. A more fascinating view it would be difficult to find. When in Venice, I pass hours leaning on the cushioned window-sill, staring down at the motley crowd of human beings and pigeons. That afternoon, a pretty girl really was feeding the *colombi*, and a tall young man really did come out of Florian's and join her. But it was my imagination only that turned him into a ghost.

Casanova was an adventurer by choice and by necessity. His life-story is a long one (the famous Memoirs are in twelve volumes). Leaving aside his boyhood and first youth, he embraced almost as many professions as he did women (the number of his love affairs accredited to him is 116). He began by studying law and was, in turn, a journalist (or what corresponded to one, in those days), an abbé, a preacher, a soldier, a violinist in an orchestra, a diplomat, a financier, a cabbalist, an alchemist, a duellist, a writer, but nothing for very long except a *coureur de femmes*, running after women till the end of his days. The scenes of his adventures—erotic, or otherwise— are all over Europe: convents in Venice and Avignon, a harem in Constantinople, royal domains in Warsaw, Potsdam and St. Petersburg, rich burgher houses in Amsterdam, peasants' cottages in Italy and moujik's hovels in Russia.

He was not in the least ashamed of having been imprisoned in, or expelled from, half the countries in Europe. Such are the hazards of an adventurer's career. And indeed, his daring flight from the *Piombi* in Venice (of which his account was published in his lifetime) invested him with a romantic halo and made a hero of him in Parisian society. It even won for him the protection of Madame de Pompadour. Doubtless it was this good fortune that procured him the post of a director of state lotteries; a post connected with the new device by which the State hoped to make millions.

Those were his most fortunate years, and had he kept within limits, they might have continued. But any permanent residence or employment were as alien to Casanova's nature as love within the marriage tie. The only repetition that never tired him was that of love with no other inhibitions than those set by caprice. He began to get into trouble with dishonoured promissory notes and a suspicion of forgery. Then came the deception practised on the aged Madame d'Urfé.

This was a very rich old lady who put her faith in occult sciences and what she called 'the hermetic secret'. She was an admirer of the alchemist Paracelsus. When Casanova first went to her house, she showed him a lighted stove on which she had kept burning, during fifteen years, a material that was intended to effect the transmutation of all metals into gold.

Casanova said of her: 'I believed these infatuations to be incurable, so why try to disillusion her? If I had not deceived her, others would have done so.'

He persuaded her that she was pregnant (at seventy-six!), but that she would die before giving birth to a son, in whom she would be reincarnated. It was essential that she should not be buried. All this does not make sense, and it is hardly to be wondered at that the old lady's heir, Monsieur de Châtelet, declared his grandmother to be a lunatic and Casanova a swindler. Nor was he content with the assurance that the Italian never took money from Madame d'Urfé: only jewels that were necessary for his experiments.

The episode is mentioned in the Memoirs of the old Marquis de Créqui, who writes of Madame d'Urfé:

Elle a fini par tomber dans les mains d'un imposteur italien, nommé Casanova, lequel avait la délicatesse de ne jamais lui demander de l'argent, mais seulement des riches pierreries, pour en former des constellations. La délicatesse de son procédé n'avait pas eu l'art de plaire à MM. de Châtelet, qui étaient les héritiers de Madame d'Urfé, et qui firent chasser Casanova du royaume.

An order, signed by the King himself, requested Casanova to leave Paris within a few days, and France, within a few months. The old roving existence began again. But the wanderer was no longer young.

Both the self-denial of the ascetic and 'the primrose path of dalliance' may lead to a lonely old age. Casanova, adventurer and libertine, was fortunate in this respect. After serving as Secretary in Vienna to the Venetian Ambassador, Foscarini, he found himself, after the latter's death, in dire straits. But the rich Count Waldstein, whom he had met in Paris and who was a nephew of his friend Prince Charles de Ligne, took compassion on him and appointed him to be his librarian in the Castle of Dux in Bohemia. Casanova was then in his sixtieth year. He passed the time contentedly enough, dabbling in alchemy with his host and writing. On one occasion, however, he got bored with country-life and fled to Vienna, in search of adventure. The escapade ended unfortunately, so he returned to the shelter of Count Waldstein's hospitable roof and the compilation of those recollections that were destined—so he wrote to Giancarlo Grimani—to be 'a school of morals'. Casanova would make statements like this, and laugh as he made them, so that one did not know whether to take them seriously, or not. When he died, in 1798, his last words were 'I lived as a philosopher, and I die as a Christian'.

It should be kept in mind that, in Casanova's days, alchemy was considered a part of philosophy. And there was in it something more than a deluded manifestation of a thirst for gold and the elixir of life; it represented the first intelligent union of chemistry with medicine.

The Italian poet, Ugo Foscolo, who passed the last eleven years of his life in England, wrote (in 1827) an article on Casanova for the *Westminster Gazette*. In this, he falls into an error that was shared at the time by many people: the strange error of assuming that Casanova never existed, and that his Memoirs were mere fiction, like those of the Baron von Munchausen. Their author—so it was said—might well be Stendhal, who—as an ironist—would have been capable of inventing such an improbable character. Foscolo was much astonished to learn that the libertine, whom he had spoken of as *un personaggio ideale,* had really been flesh and blood.

Lasciva est nobis pagina, vita proba est. . . . Casanova can hardly be taken seriously when he claims to be a respectable member of society. But, on the whole, he could afford to be sincere. In his last years he had nothing to strive for and nothing to hide. He had no more enemies, or even friends; he could afford to laugh at human weaknesses.

His is the ever-recurring type of a resourceful adventurer, who charms and seduces with his mingled wit, shrewdness, gaiety and philosophic reflection. On the stage of life, Casanova played the part of the amiable hypocrite. He might have pronounced the famous panegyric on hypocrisy, in the fifth act of Molière's *Festin de Pierre:*

> *Il n'y a plus de honte maintenaint à celà; l'hypocrisie est un vice à la mode, et tous les vices à la mode passent pour vertus. Le personnage de l'homme de bien est le meilleur de tous les personnages qu'on puisse jouer. Aujourd'hui, la profession d'hypocrite a de merveilleux avantages. C'est un art de qui l'imposture est toujours respectée; et, quoiqu'on le découvre, on n'ose rien dire contre elle.*

In the play, these lines are pronounced by Don Juan, who was what Foscolo called *un personaggio ideale,* born of a Spanish legend, to inspire poets, like Byron, or musicians, like Mozart. And Casanova was not unlike him. He possessed a charm that even fascinated Pope Clement XIII (the Venetian Rezzonico), who invested him with the Order of the Golden Spur, that

Casanova wore in diamonds and rubies. Prince Czartorysky chaffed him for taking such baubles seriously, but they were useful to impress the crowd. So was the addition of 'de Seingault' to his name (a bright idea of his own).

Given a different morality from that generally accepted, there follows, not disorder and confusion, but a different kind of order and of orthodoxy. Casanova must be judged, not by contemporary standards, or by those of the Inquisitors who imprisoned him in the *Piombi*, but by the standards of society in the days of Louis XV, which Molière and Goldoni ridiculed and which ended by drawing upon itself the excesses of the French Revolution, and songs like *Ça ira*. . . .

Casanova loved his Venice, and his ghost will haunt Rialto, as he describes it, on an early morning in 1755: the butchers arranging their shops; the fruit-stands and the stands for the sale of crockery; the purple of grapes and figs, the gold of yellow gourds; the fish-baskets, wet and sparkling, and the bronzed limbs of boatmen. Many writers have lingered in that early-morning market. Casanova sees it with the jaded looks of a gambler, who comes from the Ridotto, where he has lost all he had, plus 500 sequins on his word. . . .

That market on Rialto has been called 'the larder of Venice', whereas St. Mark's is the drawing-room. It is not in the larder that you are most likely to meet the ghost of Casanova. But someday you may imagine yourself entering a room all gilding, mirrors and cut-velvet; and, in the air, a faint perfume of amber. He will welcome you there, with his usual affability, and invite you to sit at a folding card-table, with cabriole legs and claw feet. He will take the seat opposite and lay a pack of cards before you, asking with the politest inflection:

'Shall we cut?'

At this point, I advise you to be careful. Not that you will be dealing with a card-cheat: merely with a far more experienced gambler than yourself. . . .

13

SANDRINO GUICCIOLI
AND THE GHOST OF AN
OLD SCANDAL

Blonds cheveux, sourcils bruns, front vermeil ou pâli
Dante aimait Béatrix—Byron la Guiccioli.

ALFRED DE MUSSET—*Mardoche*

THERE were three brothers Guiccioli of Mother's generation, living when I was a boy: Alessandro (or 'Sandrino', already mentioned in these pages), Ferdinando, who married an English girl whom he met in our house, and Guido. These were grandsons of the former Alessandro, husband of Teresa, beloved of Byron.

In a previous book of mine,[1] I described a visit I paid to Sandrino and his wife, in Tokyo, in 1914 (he was then Ambassador to Japan). This is what I said of my hosts:

'The Guiccioli *ménage* was a survival of a world that has passed away, and though the romance was lacking that began in the Countess Benzon's *salon* (where Byron and Teresa met), the mentality of my old friends was not so very dissimilar from that in the elder Alessandro's day. Theirs was a world of simple dignity, with an outlook on life that was both benevolent and humorous, just as theirs was a tolerance of human frailties that asked only, if trangress we must, that we should do so gracefully. A deep appreciation of beauty, especially in women, led them to recognize a lady's beauty as an attenuating

[1] *Laughing Diplomat* (John Murray—London 1938), p. 132.

circumstance, whereas to fall from grace with an ugly woman might be judged a mortal sin.'

Sandrino kept a diary, beginning in 1874. He published some extracts of it in the *Nuova Antologia*, putting them as a sequel to the previous history of his family. The Byronic scandal (for such it was considered in his family) figures incidentally. Four years after his death, I was given the diaries and other papers to look over. By that time, there was little of ancient history (that is to say up to the middle of the last century) that needed to be expurgated or bowdlerized.

Since I first saw them in the original manuscript, Sandrino's Memoirs have been published in Italian and quoted and reviewed in other languages. They form part of the voluminous literature that deals with the Byronic legend. This legend has been presented to the reading public in all its aspects, political, social and erotic. Only the attitude of the Guiccioli family has remained a negative one, deploring what to-day we call an 'excessive publicity'.

A certain reticence has been observed in the publication of Sandrino's Memoirs. As I remember his diary—in not very legible handwriting, filling innumerable little exercise-books, such as young people use at school—it contains candid and caustic comments on more than one Venetian scandal. Even the love-affair of Ignazio Guiccioli (the diarist's father, and step-son of Teresa) with a well-known society lady is treated with startling candour, and could not be published, even to-day, without giving offence to the descendants of the interested parties.

Sandrino himself was a figure in the diplomatic and social world of his time, no less interesting than that of his grandfather. (Doubtless their two ghosts haunt the Rialto.) In his youth, he had been a minor secretary in the office of Cavour, in Turin, and had considerable difficulty in understanding what his famous chief said, when giving hurried instructions in the Piedmontese dialect. His outlook on politics and on society were those of the old diplomacy, though expressed with rather more freedom than is usual in diplomatic circles.

I remember him passing through Vienna, when I was attached to our embassy there. We dined together at Sacher's. There was also, at table with us, a German relation of the Marchesa's, one of the 'Mediatized Princes', whose sovereignty had survived the Congress of Vienna. Sandrino asked me how my Chief, Duke Avarna, was getting on, and added that he had been Ambassador in Vienna for a great number of years.

'The Emperor Franz Josef is fond of him,' I explained, 'so our government does not wish to replace him.'

Sandrino exclaimed: 'Poor Emperor! His son committed suicide at Mayerling; brother Maximilian was shot by revolutionists in Mexico, and the Empress Elisabeth was murdered by an anarchist at Geneva. Franz Josef has survived these tragedies, but if Avarna were to be replaced by some other Ambassador, his heart would not bear the shock; he would not survive!'

Sandrino had no great opinion of the Duke of Avarna's capabilities, and doubtless would have liked to be ambassador in Vienna himself!

I realize that, in the subsequent conversation, I showed myself unbearably tactless and conceited. But I transcribe it, as it gives the atmosphere.

'By the way,' said the Marchesa Olga, 'I see from the papers that the young Princess . . . is here, a guest of the Archduke Frederick and his Archduchess. Have you seen her?'

The name she mentioned was that of a young royalty: a pleasant and amiable girl, but not regal, or even very distinguished in appearance.

I answered: 'Yes, I've danced with her at the *Bal bei Hof*.'

'What is she like?'

'A good cook!'

I had hardly pronounced the words when I regretted them. For all I knew, the Mediatized Prince might be a relation. He stared down his nose at me, with evident contempt, and asked:

'Why do you say "good"?'

So, that time, I escaped unscathed.

I have mentioned my friendship with the Guiccioli family in order to make it clear that it was from them that I first heard the story of Byron and Teresa. Their version may not be confirmed in every particular by other sources. As I heard it, it may not be all the truth and nothing but the truth. When one speaks of a love affair and the relations between lovers, the truth is known to two people only, and even they regard it from different points of view. More often than not, the judgment of others is apt to be pharisaical, or mawkishly tender, or almost too pedantically matter-of-fact.

The following is the story as I learnt it from Sandrino. It is natural that he should consider it from a different angle from that of an impartial biographer. What I like about his version is that, cynical as he doubtless was, and admitting a family bias, his sympathy is with the lovers, no less than with his own grandfather and namesake. He falls under the spell of the love-story; he feels the charm that surrounds it, like the perfume of long-dead roses in a vase of pot-pourri.

*   *   *

Alessandro Guiccioli the elder, grandfather of the diarist, was nearing his sixtieth year when, in January 1818, he married the seventeen-year-old daughter of his friend, Count Ruggero Gamba, who—like the bridegroom—had his family head-quarters at Ravenna. This was old Guiccioli's third matrimonial venture. His second wife had died a year before, leaving seven children. The boys were sent to a school for the sons of noblemen, the daughters to the Salesian nuns of Santa Chiara in Venice. The first meeting between Alessandro Guiccioli and his future bride occurred in Count Gamba's house. The question of a marriage having been discussed between the two elderly cronies, the girl was sent for. Guiccioli was short-sighted and the room was growing dark. So he took up a candle and walked round her, very much as if he were buying a piece of furniture.

Notwithstanding such a prosaic beginning of her courtship, Teresa was by no means averse to the marriage. She was one of many brothers and sisters in a family not overburdened with wealth. In those days, girls looked forward to matrimony as the only means of escape from a life of restraint and boredom. Despite his age, Guiccioli was a fine upstanding man, living in considerable state, cultured and pleasant to talk to. In our day—if not in his own—we would call him a reprobate. He was also eccentric, this was hardly a failing in times when to be eccentric was, among rich noblemen, rather the rule than the exception.

In the first months of her married life, Teresa appeared brimful of happiness; she sparkled, she effervesced. A letter of hers to her husband, who had been obliged to leave her for a few days, begins:

Pesaro—July 17, 1818

My adorable Spouse and Friend,—You are all my soul, the greatest happiness that I have on earth . . . without you I feel that I could not live. . . .

The evenings here pass very languidly; some small outing and then conversation with old people and priests.

I have still the five *scudi* you gave me, and I hope that on your return you will be pleased with my economy.

My cough is quite gone, without need of medicines. And you, my Dear, be careful of the scirocco in Rimini, and of the heat, and of the night airs on your return. . . . Continue to love me and be sure that you never could have found a bride more loving and more sincere than your

T.G.G.

There is no truth in the statement, accepted by André Maurois, that from the first days of their marriage, Guiccioli and his wife occupied separate apartments. Nor—considering his subsequent achievements—can it have been true that *'un vieillard, même cultivé, ne pouvait satisfaire cette jeune femme'*. At sixty, and even at a more advanced age, Guiccioli was far from being *'un vieillard'*.

In the autumn of 1818, he took his wife to Venice, where they passed the winter. Byron had already been living there some two years. This is how he makes his first appearance in Sandrino's commentary:

> There dwelt in those days in Venice, George Byron: the object of infinite admiration to the women, who found him most seductive, and to the young men, who recognized in him the supreme prototype of that romantic, fatal, and satanic elegance which the changing times had made so fashionable. People of culture admired in him *l'altissimo poeta*.

> In former days, Guiccioli had been a friend of the dramatist, Vittorio Alfieri, whom Byron himself had taken as a model, in an attempt to reform the British drama by 'a severer approach to the rules'. Animated by a very similar idea, Guiccioli had discussed with Alfieri the possibility of setting up some kind of a model theatre, where the best actors might give representations of the best tragedies, both ancient and modern. With this idea in mind, Guiccioli hastened to make the acquaintance of the great English poet, and after several meetings, he introduced Byron to his wife. The presentation occurred one night in April, in the house of the Contessa Benzon, whose receptions began at midnight, after the theatres had closed. It was a case, apparently of love at first sight. Byron had the head of an Apollo. Teresa's beautiful features were framed in ringlets of the Titian bronze. They made an ideal couple.

In those days, the old custom of the *cavalier servente*, or *cicisbeo*, was still recognized as legitimate. According to the *Encyclopaedia Britannica*, the *cicisbeo* was the professed gallant of a married woman, who attended her at all public entertainments, it being considered unfashionable for her husband to be escort. This custom was characteristic of Venice in her decline.

It is probable that the *cicisbeo* was something different in each individual case; at most, a lover; at least, the lady's faithful companion and bondman. In many cases, the *cicisbei* were chosen by the bride's family, with the consent of the husband, at the moment of stipulating the marriage contract. Sometimes only one was chosen; sometimes as many as four. The *cicisbeo* accompanied the lady everywhere: to mass, on her outings, to the theatre, to the card-tables. On quiet evenings in a noble-man's house, you might find the husband in his study with the classics, the wife in her boudoir with the *cicisbei*. Old Alessandro Guiccioli would certainly have raised no objection to his wife's relation with Lord Byron had they remained within the limits prescribed by custom, even though the poet's outstanding personality, his social position and great fame, made him less adapted to the role of *cavalier servente* than the usual young man about town. But Byron was too casual in the conduct of his love-affairs, too ignorant of, or indifferent to, decorum; Teresa was too proud of having made a conquest of *il mio Byron* (to call him this openly was a foolish breach of etiquette) and she could not refrain from boasting. It was only when they blatantly exceeded the bounds prescribed for such situa-tions, that the husband betrayed his resentment and began to consider the possibility of a legal separation from his wife. Teresa's own family, the Gambas, had no qualms. They fostered an intrigue that appeared to them flattering to their daughter and sister.

It was on the occasion of the lovers' first separation, when Teresa had to accompany her husband to his estates at Isola d'Ariano, that Byron wrote the *Stanzas to the River Po* that begins:

> River that rollest by the ancient walls
> Where dwells the lady of my love . . .

and contains the lines:

> A stranger loves a lady of the land,
> Born far beyond the mountains, but his blood
> Is all meridian. . . .

Before those marshy lands on the delta of the river had been reclaimed, they used to breed fevers, and Teresa fell ill, Guiccioli took her to Ravenna. This is what his grandson, a century later, had to say about the matter:

Our property at the Ca' Zen, where the fair Teresa had to pass a few tedious days, was a dreary spot; the air was not healthy and tertian fevers not infrequent. Apparently she caught them and pretended, or really believed herself to be *in extremis,* so that on reaching Ravenna, she wrote a letter to her lover which would have drawn tears from a stone. Byron, who was anxious to continue the adventure, left Venice on June 2, and reached Ravenna on the 10th. [*N.B. Eight days to do about 100 miles does not betray a great haste!*] He took up his quarters at an inn not far from the tomb of Dante. On hearing of his arrival, my grandfather went to call, and finding him so badly lodged, offered the hospitality of his own house. It was the natural thing in Romagna, in those days, and not unusual to-day, to offer and to accept hospitality among friends and acquaintances, for the inns, both then and now, were so unspeakably bad as to be intolerable for a person of quality. My grandfather's offer has been considered surprising by many people, especially by foreigners, but if he had not made it, he would have violated the rules of the most elementary hospitality, as laid down by local custom and in view of his personal relations with Lord Byron.

On the occasion of his marriage, my grandfather had reorganized his household with considerable state, at least according to the ideas of the time and in Romagna: many servants, many courses at dinner, many horses and carriages in the stables. That he should place them at the disposal of his guest need cause no surprise, since the horses were there.[1] Indeed, on more formal occasions,

[1] It appears however that Byron was not impressed. Of Guiccioli he writes that he was a very polite personage, 'but I wish he would not carry me out in his Coach-and-Six, like Whittington and his Cat!'
Few towns in the world have seen such changes as Ravenna—once capital of the Roman Empire. The Ravenna described by Guiccioli has long disappeared as a social and cultural centre, with the disappearance of the noble families: the Lovatellis, the Rasponis, the Guicciolis, who have gone elsewhere, or died out, only the Pasolinis remain.

the carriages used to be preceded by outriders, or *coureurs* (we, ourselves, called them *volanti*). I remember as a child having played with certain strange old caps, four-cornered like the biretta of a priest, made of white and blue silk, much faded with age and ornamented with what had once been feathered plumes, also blue and white. This was all that remained of the liveries of my grandfather's *coureurs*. Such luxury in the family equipage was still customary in Italy after the French Revolution, and it lasted longer in the provinces than in the big towns.

Of what nature were the relations between Byron and the Guiccioli during the six or seven weeks when they were together at Ravenna? He imagined, or let it be believed, that in order to meet with his lady-love he committed follies, had adventures and faced dangers, compared to which those of Don Juan were child's play. I make bold to cast a doubt on all this melodrama. One must be ignorant of what Ravenna was like in those days, and of the habits of a lady of quality, to believe that such escapades could have been possible. Add to this that my grandfather was diffident and meticulous, and that Teresa, despite her youth, was not a woman to lose her head or to run unnecessary risks. Lastly it should be remembered that husband and wife shared their board and bed. Therefore, the meetings between the lovers must have taken place very quietly, in the house of a complaisant friend, or as I have been assured—in the home of her parents. To what extent they favoured the intrigue was made clear by the law-suit that followed.

Other flights of phantasy and further dreams of a foreigner, who knew but little of our ways and was steeped in the romantic follies of a school which imagined that Italy, in 1819, was still that of the Borgias and the Farneses, brought Byron to believe that, at any moment he might have been hurled down to death through a trap-door, or stabbed in the back by myrmidons of the house of Guiccioli.

Scenes of violent jealousy were not admitted in certain classes of society, and they were put down to eccentricity and ill-breeding. It is sufficient to point out that when my grandfather gave his wife a severe scolding and ordered her to modify her habits and her behaviour, she turned on him with bitter reproaches—as her numerous apologists have testified—because she alone, of all the ladies of Romagna, was expected to do without a lover. Public opinion was by no means surprised that for some months my grandfather should have ignored, or pretended to ignore, the intrigue, for such conduct was expected of a man of wit and breeding. But it raised a fine outcry when, contrary to all precedent, my grandfather set the law in motion in a suit for adultery! Then indeed did everyone accuse him of being an unbalanced and barbarous husband!

14

POLITICS AND POETRY

Lady! if for the cold and cloudy clime
Where I was born, but where I would not die,
Of the great Poet-Sire of Italy
I dare to build the imitative rhyme,
Harsh Runic copy of the South's sublime,
Thou art the cause. . . .

BYRON—Dedication of *The Prophecy of Dante*

WHEN a poet takes to politics and to adventure, inspired by a national ideal, many people consider him a hero, and an equal number look upon him as a nuisance.

This happened to Byron and, a century later, to d'Annunzio.

Whereas in the eighteen-twenties Venice was under Austrian domination, Ravenna was part of the Papal States, and as such ruled by ecclesiastics.

The reigning Pope was Pius VII (Chiaramonti): the same Pope who had been kept in exile in France by Napoleon I. His Secretary of State was the reactionary Cardinal Consalvi.

In Ravenna there was a clerical faction, claiming to represent law and order, and a Liberal faction, aiming at revolution. Alessandro Guiccioli was on good terms with the clerics, whereas Teresa's family, the Gambas, were counted among the liberals.

As Byron put it: 'The police is all on the alert, and the Cardinal glares pale through all his purple! . . . I vaticinate a *row* in Italy, in which case, I don't know that I won't have a finger in it. I dislike the Austrians and think the Italians infamously oppressed.'

Those were the first birth-throes of the Risorgimento: revolutionary movements destined to failure, the times not yet being ripe for them. French occupation had left a ferment of new ideas in the Italian provinces. For a time, Austrian soldiery and Papal police could press the lid down on a pot that was beginning to boil. But not for long.

Had Byron been there at a later period, he might have been numbered among the makers of United Italy. Instead of which, he sacrificed his life for the liberation of Greece from Turkish misrule. Thus he rehabilitated himself in the eyes of his countrymen. He even influenced the foreign policy of his country, that policy which led, a few years later, to the battle of Navarino, and to all that followed therefrom.[1]

Meanwhile, the love-affair with Teresa began to figure in political reports, addressed by the Papal Legate in Romagna to the Holy See. These reports are now in the Vatican archives. They speak of Byron as 'one of the political supporters of romanticism', and request that something be done to rid Ravenna of his presence, not only on account of his political activities, but because he caused grave scandal among the noble families of Ravenna.

This was true enough, for—as we saw in the preceding chapter—matters had come to a head between old Guiccioli and Teresa. The latter—as Sandrino points out—was in the habit, whenever she wanted to get her own way, of feigning ill-health. So it was 'on the advice of Doctor Aglietti' that, during her husband's absence, she accompanied Byron to a villa he had rented at La Mira. The maladies mentioned to justify this escapade are not usually associated with romantic adventure. It was from La Mira that she wrote the following letter to her husband, the date being 30th September 1819:

MY DEAREST ALESSANDRO,—You have seen the letter which I wrote to Papà. I am glad of this, but you must not think that if I do not mention my health to him that I must be quite well. On

[1] See *Byron, the Last Journey*, Harold Nicolson (Constable 1924).

the contrary, during the last few days I have been troubled with hemorroids, a most distressing malady, and I suffer also from headaches and a return of my cough. For these last maladies, I have been advised to take a journey, but before deciding, I must think the matter over. . . . I am still here, at La Mira, a most delightful spot, where one can live, as I do, in the greatest retirement, without being at all bored.

I cannot tell you how kind Milord is! He has had a piano brought here for me, and music, and no end of books. Then there is his company, which is so precious that, if I only had my health, I could have nothing left to wish for. Byron sends you his greetings and is sorry that in your last letter there should have been no word for him. I am grieved to hear that you have so many worries. . . .

For cool impudence, this letter—and others like it—would be hard to beat, and it is truly remarkable as being written by a young woman who had not yet passed her nineteenth year and had been brought up in a convent.

The inevitable crisis was postponed because it appeared that Byron was about to leave for England. A visit from Tom Moore, the Irish poet, had filled him with a desire to go home. He meant to take his little daughter, Allegra, with him. The date fixed for their departure had arrived. In front of the Nani-Mocenigo palace, a gondola full of luggage rocked gently on the wavelets of the Grand Canal. Byron was ready. He had put on his gloves. Allegra was on board. All he had to do was to step in, but he waited for his guns. At that moment he swore that if the clock struck one before his guns were placed in the gondola, he would not start at all. The hour struck, and he remained. That night he wrote to Teresa that love had conquered; he would come back to her.

So Byron went to Ravenna for the second time, on 20th January 1820.

Meanwhile, Guiccioli, after a stormy interview with Teresa, had arrived at a tentative understanding with her, based on a written agreement, a specially prepared schedule for his wife's behaviour. (He had prepared a schedule, a series of 'maxims', also for his first wife, the Contessa Placidia Zinanni, who had brought him a large dowry. In her case, there never had been any question of infidelity.) The document was accepted by Teresa, with some amendments introduced in the original text. The articles in Guiccioli's charter were twenty-one; Teresa's amendments were eleven, the first and second of which read as follows: 'To get up in the morning, when I please.' 'To receive any visitor who may happen to call.'

It was the custom in those days in Italy, and more especially in the Papal States, to draw up an elaborate pre-nuptial settlement, mapping out in detail the future married life of an engaged couple. The wife's right to a daily drive was carefully set down, as well as her right to a box at the theatre. Guiccioli's charter for Teresa was a similar but much more elaborate document, and it had obviously been drawn up to meet a special case. Article 11 reads as follows:

> She shall always be willing to live in such a place as shall be convenient, in view of her husband's circumstances; and she shall therefore keep her things in good order, ready to start or to return, giving up all wild ideas for journeys and sojourns that should not be convenient to her husband and the family.

There is much in the document, prepared by Guiccioli, to show Teresa what he expected of her, that the average husband might read with sympathy, and the average wife with dismay. Leaving apart the details, the special object to be obtained by Teresa's acceptance (even with amendments) was a complete rupture of her relations with Byron.

Yet there he was again, back in Ravenna.

The snow lay deep on the plain and in the pine-forests, where he had ridden with Teresa. But the town was gay, for carnival was at its height, and Byron, during the first weeks of his stay, let politics alone and dedicated himself to the lady, assuming once more the part of *cavalier servente*. Everyone made much of them and seemed pleased to welcome so handsome a couple. Even old Guiccioli appeared resigned, though in his heart a new design was maturing. Better to accomplish his purpose, he consented that Byron should occupy the upper floor of his palace. It was convenient that the correspondent in a possible action for legal separation should be lodged where his every movement could be watched and noted down for future reference.

So Byron left the inn and took up his abode in what was than called the 'Palazzo Osi'. He kept four horses, four carriages, six servants and a small menagerie. His bedroom, with frescoed walls, looked out on the courtyard. His working-room, where he wrote 'Cain', 'Marino Faliero' and 'Sardanapalus', was on the front of the house and looked out on the street. The old manservant, Filippo Allegri, spoke of his master as 'that crazy Lord' and marvelled that so important a patrician should have his rooms full of dogs, cats and monkeys, and should seek adventures with the most humble women, even the poor girls who went barefoot to gather wood in the forest.

When Guiccioli had collected all the proofs he required, he asked the ecclesiastical courts for a legal separation based on motives of adultery.

Despite the outcry raised by the Gambas, the sentence from Rome allowed the plea, with the obligation, on the husband's part, of paying a small alimony; on the part of the wife, of returning to the home of her parents. Thus the fair Countess left her husband's house and went to stay in the villa of the Gambas at Filetto, fifteen miles out of Ravenna, where the intrigue continued.

But Byron was getting tired of it.

More than in the love-affair his interests centred in the fact that Romagna and other parts of Italy were preparing for insurrection, whereas the Princes of the Holy Alliance were meeting at Laybach and consulting as to the best means of maintaining their power.

Count Gamba's villa at Filetto was a meeting place for the local sect of the Carbonari (a word meaning 'charcoal-burners', and corresponding to certain secret societies of a revolutionary tendency that played an active part in the history of Italy and of France in the nineteenth century). The members who conspired in Ravenna called themselves 'Bersaglieri Americani', and elected Byron as their chief. The fact of his being a foreigner of so much fame and distinction made it difficult for the police to curb his activities. His apartment became the arsenal where arms were deposited.

But the persecutions of the Papal authorities obliged the Gambas to take refuge in Florence. In what was then the Grand Duchy of Tuscany, they felt safe. Byron refused to follow them (or the lady), and at the end of October 1821, started for Pisa and Genoa.

Not quite three years later, he sailed on the *Hercules*, for Cephalonia.

Teresa then found herself abandoned for good and all, and what was worse, with such limited means that she was in danger of facing real poverty. So she made herself out as repentant and full of remorse; she begged her husband's forgiveness and brought into play all the wiles that a clever and beautiful woman knows how to use. In the end, she persuaded Guiccioli to take her back into his home. The reconciliation did not last long, but when the ill-assorted couple separated once more, the allowance made to Teresa was much more liberal.

She was still with Guiccioli when, one morning, her stepson, Ignazio (father of Sandrino) brought her the news of Byron's death at Missolonghi. She was in bed, and turned her face to the wall for a few minutes, without speaking. And that was all.

*   *   *

One of those essays that Chesterton used to write for the *Daily News* and the *Spectator* was about the Optimism of Byron.

He pointed out that Byron's sensational popularity was founded on his pessimism, in an age of sentiment that was largely artificial.[1]

Characteristically combative and dogmatic, G.K.C. denies both the pessimism and the artificiality, and goes on to say:

> Everything is against our appreciating the spirit and the age of Byron. . . . His world seems a sad and faded world, where men were romantic in whiskers, ladies lived, apparently, in bowers, and the very word has the sound of a piece of stage scenery. Roses and nightingales recur in their poetry with the monotonous elegance of a wall-paper pattern. . . .
>
> But the more shrewdly and earnestly we study the histories of men, the less ready shall we be to make use of the word 'artificial'. Many customs, many dresses, many works of art are branded with artificiality because they exhibit vanity and self-consciousness: as if vanity were not a deep and elemental thing, like love and hate and the fear of death.
>
> Byron's pessimism may or may not have been the real thing, but it is probable that he really was often sick of the life he led and of himself. Such are the trials of an egotist who is also a poet. He alternates between the older elements of the cosmos and the latest fripperies of society: between the desert and the fashionable restaurant.

G.K.C. concludes:

> The truth is that Byron was one of a class who may be called the unconscious optimists. . . . In Greece he heard the cry of reality and at the time when he was dying, he began to live. He heard suddenly the call of that buried and sub-conscious happiness which is in all of us, and which may emerge suddenly at the sight of the grass of a meadow or the spears of the enemy.

We can accept this conclusion which may indeed embody a profound truth under the seeming contradiction of a paradox. For my part I am content to conclude by quoting Sandrino

[1] Reprinted in *Twelve Types* (Arthur L. Humphreys, London 1903).

Guiccioli's commentaries on the end of the story. His is the quiet, sophisticated wisdom of the aristocrat and elderly man of the world, speaking of an old scandal in his own family.

This is how he describes his grandfather, the elder Alessandro, who in his old age, went to live in Venice:

> Every evening, he would go to some theatre, but on account of his failing eyesight, he had to be accompanied by a young clerk, or secretary, and he wished the young man to be let in without paying. The Impresario naturally refused. What do you suppose my grandfather did then? Having discovered that the unfortunate Impresario had signed several promissory notes, he bought them up and threatened him with legal proceedings and a debtor's prison. The Impresario could not pay, but allowed my grandfather's clerk free entrance to the theatre. The promissory notes had cost the price of the tickets twenty times over. But my grandfather had his way, which was all he cared about. With him, the passion for the theatre soon became a sort of mania. Not only did he go there every evening, whatever the performance might be, but he might be seen also in the daytime, in the open squares, on the Riva degli Schiavoni, watching the puppet shows. In order not to attract the attention of the crowd, he would wrap his cloak round him, to hide the cross of the Order of St. Stephen, worn round his neck.

> But in Venice everyone knew and recognized him, not only by his commanding presence and great height and the Orders that were rarely seen even on persons of distinction, but also for a strange visor of green satin which he wore over his forehead to shade his eyes from the glare.

Sandrino's comments on Teresa are mostly severe: a lady of quality may have her lovers—it is understood—but she should not lose her head or her dignity. And Teresa did both. But in the end he speaks of her with a gentle kindliness and comprehension:

> The youthful Teresa, aged nineteen, beautiful as an angel, born and bred in the moral and social atmosphere of Italy at the beginning

of the century, married for convenience' sake to an old noble-man forty years her senior, meets with a young man of great lineage, handsome as an Apollo, vigorous as a Hercules, expert in all the arts of seduction, as in the exercises of the mind and body. He is surrounded by an aureole of glory and preceded by the fame of strange adventures. That she should have fallen to his fascinations is in the natural order of things. A repulse on her part to Byron's advances, in Venice, in the salon of the Benzon, in the year of grace 1819, would have made her worthy of being wor-shipped on our altars or shut up in an asylum. She was not compounded of the material of which saints are made. Nor was she insane. She was a woman, like so many others, such as the times and her surroundings had made her.

Byron himself was not a good, pious and virtuous young man, such as the fair Countess had tried to describe in certain Memoirs of her own, nor was he the monster that some bilious puritan English old-maid (more hysterical than intelligent) has tried to make us believe. He was, as we should say nowadays, neurasthenic, excessive and extravagant to a point which at times makes him appear almost mad, but with all the qualities and the defects that blend so strangely in natures such as his.

Easily carried away by his enthusiasms, lacking in moral sense . . . with intense physical desires and all the means of satisfying them; rich, handsome, highly born, flattered and admired, he had given himself up to pleasure when such faults are frequent and excusable even in those who never had such tempta-tions, or possessed his soaring genius. That on meeting a beautiful woman, he should have loved her and made love to her and wandered over Italy in her company is all quite natural and needs no abstruse explanation.

At the beginning, their love was sincere and passionate, such as both Teresa and Byron were worthy of inspiring. All this lasted till October 1819, that is to say, till the days spent at La Mira. Later, as often happens, things began to change. Teresa, who was a woman of quick intelligence and a reflective disposition, began to feel that she was risking her fortune and her social position. Nor could she foresee that in time, some rays from the poet's glory would form an aureole round her fair head. Byron's nature was not easy; his mode of living was bizarre, so that life with him was not always pleasant. As he was incapable of dissimulation, it is probable that he did not hide the fact that his bonds were sometimes irksome.

Be that as it may, it is a fact that Teresa was not much upset when Byron left for Greece, nor when she learnt of his death. Indeed, she was prompt in finding consolation. The French actress, Mademoiselle Déjazet, on hearing that the Empress Marie Louise had married again, exclaimed:

'*Sale Autrichienne!* If I had touched the great man, only with the tips of my fingers, I would never again have washed my hand!' We know that our little Countess washed her hands.

In the first days, Byron loved her, as I said before, with an overwhelming passion. He was too fine a nature, too generous, too great a gentleman, not to realise that this love was different from the greater part of those other loves which hitherto had filled his adventurous existence. Here was a young woman of his own class, beautiful and sweet, in the springtime of life, and he had fired her imagination and compromised her position, so that when he would have been willing to sever the chains that were growing heavy, he felt he could not do so unless he justified himself in his own eyes and in those of the world, by interposing between himself and her the broad expanse of sea and a great ideal, such as that of the liberation of Greece.

Some will quote a phrase or two from a letter, or mention some passing infidelity, to argue that Byron never loved the Guiccioli. They prove only that they have little knowledge of the human heart and none of love.

To speak with indifference, with sceptical contempt, to one's friends, of one's own passions, even when they are gnawing at one's heart, to deny the existence of love at the moment when it gives the greatest torment, this is merely one of those contradictions, one of those attitudes that men indulge in most frequently, even when they are not poets and do not live in a period of romanticism. From Don Juan, passing by Namouna to Monsieur de Camors, how many examples of this style have there been, and how many disciples. . . .

What influence, literary, religious or moral, did the Guiccioli exert over Byron? Very little, to my mind. She was too young and inexperienced to be able to give advice on literary matters to such a man. And it should be kept in mind that, in the days of their love-affair, she knew no English. As to religion, she had too little herself to be able to give any to others, and so, too, with morality.

Certainly, a beautiful woman, clever and beloved, must always exercise some influence, and it is possible that she may have suggested some theme for his songs (as with *The Prophecy of Dante*). It is also possible that she may have fed the fires of his love for Italy, and his desire for her liberation. She may have succeeded in erasing from his poems some small obscenity, some phrase that was shocking to the orthodox. But we have no proof that even Laura, or Beatrice, did more than this.

15

THE MASKS

Excellent Sir,—I take up my pen and lay aside the false nose I have been wearing night and day for close on a week, to make a communication which will doubtless interest you as it has profoundly affected me. . . .

This letter is quoted in Sir Arthur Quiller Couch's romance, *Sir John Constantine*. It is addressed to Gervase Arundel Esq., of Constantine in Cornwall, and dated Venice—Ash Wednesday (4.30 a.m.) 1761. Only in Venice, in the eighteenth century can one imagine anyone wearing a false nose, day and night, for a week on end.

The writer—Phineas Fett—goes on to say:

. . . Close upon twelve months, I have drawn a respectable salary as Director of Public Festivities to the Sisterhood of the Conventual Body of Santa Chiara. Nor is the post a sinecure; since these estimable women, though themselves vowed against earthly delights, possess a water-side garden which, periodically, and especially in the week preceding Lent, they throw open to the public—a practice from which they derive unselfish pleasure and a useful advertisement. . . .

To anyone employed in this way, a false nose might well substitute a mask, as commonly worn in Venice during Carnival.

In most languages, the word 'mask' has more than one meaning:—a cover for the face, or the personage who, on the stage, represents a certain distinctive character, such as Harlequin, Columbine, Pulcinella (ancestor of Punch, as of Pierrot), the boastful Captain Matamoro, and so on.

Venice was the home of masks in all the meanings of the word. Anyone, at almost any time, might be seen wearing one: the beggar holding out his hand for alms; the servant-girl out shopping; the mother with her baby in her arms. No wonder that Carnival never seemed to end!

The little half-mask of white satin, the three-cornered hat (worn by women as well as by men—as Longhi's pictures show), the black cape or *bautta*, that sometimes had a hood to cover the head: these were part of a Venetian's normal get-up. The patrician might, if he chose, be recognized as such, even when masked, by wearing a cape of scarlet.

A mask went naturally with powdered hair and patches, with candle-light and the play of a fan. It was difficult to know where artifice merged into reality.

At the end of Max Beerbohm's *The Happy Hypocrite*, the Italian actress, la Gambogi, tears the waxen mask off her former lover's face, hoping to shame him before Jenny, his young wife. But there, staring back at her, is not the man she had known, but a face that is even as the mask had been. Line upon line, feature for feature, it is the same. The mask and the face were one. . . . She goes, and husband and wife are left alone in the garden. Nor lies the mask any more on the lawn, for the sun has melted it.

Here is a philosophy that appears again and again, all over the world: in Socrates and Pirandello; in Bernard Shaw and the Chinese poems of Li-po.

It is based upon a paradox, on a contrast that is a similarity: on the antithesis between fact and fiction, between reality and appearance, between what was and what we remember.

The two concepts are separated by a no-man's-land that belongs neither to the one, nor to the other, but has something of both. From that uncertain borderland arises the doubt: What is substance? What is shadow? And finally the question of Pilate: 'What is truth?'

The query arose on the Venetian stage in the eighteenth

CARLO GOLDONI, BY DAL ZETTO

ΠΑΜΕΛΑ ΥΠΑΝΔΡΟΣ

ΚΩΜΩΔΙΑ

ΚΑΡΟΛΟΥ ΓΟΛΔΟΝΙΟΥ

Νῦν πρῶτον μεταγλωττισθεῖσα παρὰ

ΦΡΑΓΚΙΣΚΟΥ ΒΑΡΕ

Καὶ ἐπιθεωρηθεῖσα παρὰ

ΣΠΥΡΙΔΩΝΟΣ ΒΛΑΝΤΗ.

ΕΝ ΒΕΝΕΤΙᾼ.

ΠΑΡΑ ΝΙΚΟΛΑῼ ΓΛΥΚΕΙ Τῼ ΕΞ ΙΩΑΝΝΙΝΩΝ.

1817.

Karolo Goldoni

century and came down to earth again in the form of a rivalry between the mask and the face. The conventional *commedia dell'arte* was beginning to retire before the naturalism of Goldoni. Performers taking the parts of Harlequin, Columbine and Pulcinella were being ousted by actors impersonating real people. The struggle, at times, was a bitter one. Goldoni's competitors waged a malicious war against his more modern plays, and even some of the actors rebelled. They had vested interests in the *maschere*, and dreaded the decline of their popularity among the masses and the princes. Had not the Emperor Mathias accorded patents of nobility to Harlequin, a fictitious personage? (Here the paradox had been carried to extremes.)

The old type of 'improvised' comedy was born in Venice in the sixteenth century, and spread all over Europe, where it was simply called 'Italian'. The same characters, the *maschere*, appeared and reappeared in different plays, and the name of the actor often disappeared in the part impersonated.

I imagine that all of us—or nearly all—have been thrilled by Harlequin, in his tight parti-coloured clothes, as we have been delighted and horrified by the disgraceful behaviour of the hook-nosed, hunch-backed Punch or Pulcinela. These were the best-known characters in the *commedia dell'arte*, but there were plenty more, from various towns in Italy, speaking with different accents, and each with his peculiarities. Besides which there were the anonymous professionals: the Doctor, the Lawyer, and the Constable who pursued Columbine's lover and is the prototype of the policeman, who gets kicked and clubbed in Christmas pantomime.

The character of Pantalone—the Venetian masque *par excellence*, who never talked anything but the Venetian dialect—was born on the islands of the Giudecca, where a small coterie of comedians first attempted the improvised dialogues that later developed into this form of burlesque comedy.

The scenes, unwritten except in skeleton, were connected by

links and ligatures (the *lazzi* of Harlequin). There was, in those times, a certain classic reluctance to admit the æsthetic dignity of comedy, as if it could never rise above buffoonery and was as hollow as a grinning mask.

In giving a new lease of life to the long dead Cyrano de Bergerac, Rostand rebelled against this conception. A comedy is no less such because it ends in disappointment and death; it may be heroic. In the hands of Dante, it can be divine. It is the power of a man's spirit that turns tragedy into comedy. And it is this power that is lacking in the *commedia dell'arte*, which remains farcical throughout. But, admitting its limitations, no one can deny its charm and its humour.

The first scenes to be put on the stage were arguments between master and servant. The servant was a poor, ignorant creature, who had come to Venice from some mountain village, in the Cadore, to sell charcoal. His clothes, face and hands were always black with coal-dust. Everyone laughed at his uncouth speech and gestures. He was called Giovanni, or Zane for short. When exported to England, he became a 'zany', meaning a character whose business it is to make sport for others.

The opposite number to Zane was a Venetian nobleman (of the decadence), a rather pompous patrician, who liked to be spoken of as '*il Magnifico*'. In time, *il Magnifico* becomes old, impoverished and crotchety. Out of this metamorphosis emerges Pantalone.

Having become stingy, with advancing years, Pantalone goes about almost in rags and in constant fear that people may steal his money (you will find him, in this guise, speaking French, in Molière's play, *L'Avare*, in the part of the miser, Arpagon). He is also inclined to be amorous in a senile way, and thus becomes the rival in love of his own son.

He is represented as a tall, thin old gentleman, with a big, hooked nose, wearing a dark grey mask. He is dressed in scarlet, with a long grey cape; a dagger at his belt, and long pointed slippers; on his head is a black and scarlet skull-cap. He is always protesting about something and his beard wags up and down, keeping time with his lamentations.

In his Magnifico days, it was his pride that he could pay for everything. Later on, he regards this as his misfortune. To-day, he impersonates the tax-payer, and *Paga Pantalone!* has become a common expression in the Italian language. It dates, apparently, from the Peace of Campoformio, that is to say from October 1717. In a book called *La Fine della Serenissima*, by Riccardo Bratti, I find an illustration representing a carriage and pair, leaving the inn at Campoformio (a village in the province of Udine). Inside the carriage are the Plenipotentiary of France (General Bonaparte) and the Plenipotentiary of Austria (the Arch-Duke Charles). The innkeeper runs after them, calling out: 'The bill! Who pays the bill?'

Bonaparte answers: 'It's not up to me.' And the Arch-Duke: 'I have no money!' But standing up behind the carriage in the place of the footman, is Pantalone. And he says to the innkeeper: *'Amigo, pago mi!'* (My friend, *I* will pay!)

Since then it has always been Pantalone's (and the tax-payer's) grievance, that it's up to him to foot the bill. In the skit on Campoformio, there is a political meaning. Peace between France and Austria was made at the expense of Venice.

I need hardly inform the reader that the tendency to create *maschere* is a very old one; so is the tendency to transform the old ones into something modern, or even to create new ones. The military braggart; or *Miles Gloriosus*, of Plautus, becomes the bombastic Capitano Matamoro, in Italy and in Spain. And what is *Charlot*, created by Charlie Chaplin but a *maschera* that might figure in the *commedia dell'arte?*

*   *   *

Into this harlequinade, there steps a quiet little man with a whimsical smile and a twinkling eye: Carlo Goldoni.

I have heard it said of him that he first adopted the *maschere* and then killed them. In a sense, this is true. He wrote some 120 plays, and in many of them he put Harlequin, Matamoro, and Pantalone, just as they had been in the *commedia dell'arte*. But he allowed them no monopoly of the stage, which he reformed in Italy, as a century before Molière had reformed it in France. For him indeed, all the world was a stage, and all the men and women merely players—or, to say it with the Greeks, *hypokritai*.

Harlequin might still come forward to the footlights, but he was only a ghost out of the past, one of many on Rialto. For Goldoni's pleasant and friendly genius, comedy lived everywhere, walked with him in the Piazza, sat and gossiped with him in the cafés, danced with him in Carnival. It was not the Venice of the Doge's Palace, robed in crimson velvet and cloth of gold. It was the Venice of the *calli* and the *campielli*, of humble and rather bare interiors, of girls who laughed and gossiped as they drew water for their kitchens, where water was not laid on! There are no 'messages' in Goldoni's plays, no social enquiries, no psychological problems to be solved. In them we find amusement, illusion, and memories of life, before the French Revolution, in a world that was happier, in many ways, than ours is to-day. The humour is piquant, but always kindly, and even his foreign women (such as the Dutch girl in *Un curioso accidente*) have a merry, mischievous artfulness that is all Venetian. We find the same homely intimacy, the same warming geniality, that Longhi puts into pictures that have none of the splendour of Tiepolo.

Goethe said of Goldoni that his play *Baruffe Chioggiotte* was created out of nothing. This facility made him extraordinarily prolific. Once he made a bet that he would produce sixteen plays in one year; another time that he would produce a play a week for a whole year. In both cases, he won the wager easily.

The second *tour de force* started with a sonnet, recited by the

prima-donna in the theatre of Sant' Angelo, on the last night of
Carnival 1750. But on the last Sunday in Carnival 1751, the
concluding play of the series had still to be written. It so
happened that, when passing under the arch at the entrance to
the Merceria, Goldoni met an old Armenian selling candied
fruits. From this chance encounter sprang the play called
Pettegolezzi delle Donne. The Armenian fruit-seller figures in
it, with the name he was known by: Albagigi. The play
was written, rehearsed and acted within a few days. One
might say it was improvised, like a dialogue in the *commedia
dell'arte*.

There is a scene in this comedy, in which Anzoletta, a
little seamstress, meets in the street, a cousin of Checchina
(who is both her client and her rival in love). She explains to
the cousin, Donna Cate, that she is taking a new frock to
Checchina, and asks to be directed on her way.

It is unlikely that such a modest seamstress would not know
the way to a client's house. But question and answer—as the
question put by Gobbo to Launcelot in a greater play—give
Goldoni the opportunity of describing a little corner of the
town.

Goldoni was a realist, the first realist in modern Italian
drama. As such, he was beloved of his fellow-citizens, who
saw themselves mirrored in his plays. They followed the
vicissitudes of their daily lives, as from the stage-box of a
modest theatre: the box, that is, from which one can watch
the play and the by-play: the actors, the prompter and the
scene-shifters. From such a vantage point, all the shabbiness
of the play-house is apparent, the grossness of the painting,
the unreality of the properties, the absurdity of the most
tragic impersonations. The virtuous wife, hotly pursued by the
villain, pauses in the wings, before rushing, in tears and desper-
ation, upon the stage. But does this destroy, or enhance, the
charm of the performance? Do we not all share a childish
longing to go behind the scenes? In Goldoni's plays, we seem

to be doing it all the time. And we enjoy both the illusion and being disillusioned.

Foreigners, doped with sentimental errors, may not find, in Goldoni, the Venice of their dreams. And they may turn back in relief—shall we say?—to Byron. What we—fellow-citizens of the play-wright—like to recognize is our beloved Venice, without the sham and the cheapness, so often emphasized in literature, but as she was, is now, and (we hope) ever shall be.

*   *   *

I possess a proof of the popularity of Goldoni in my own family. Francesco Varè, at the beginning of the last century, took it into his head to translate some of the plays. So far, there is nothing remarkable about the project. No less than eighty of the comedies have been translated into foreign tongues. But old Francesco was peculiar in his choice of a language into which to transfer Goldoni's pleasant humour. It was ancient Greek!

He got as far as translating *Pamela Nubile* and *Pamela Maritata*, and he left a copy of the second in the Venetian library that has now come to me. I only know of the existence of the first translation because it is mentioned in the Preface of ΠΑΜΕΛΑ ΥΠΑΝΔΡΟΣ.

In this Preface, it is said that the translator was encouraged to proceed in his labour of love by the success of the previous work ΠΑΜΕΛΑ ΑΝΥΠΑΝΔΟΣ, which had been produced in Vienna. He adds that it was his wish to produce these plays for the benefit of the many Greek friends and acquaintances, with whom he had established relations while trading in Asia Minor, and in Greece itself.

So far, all is clear. But the text is not easy to follow. Probably this is because it was revised by one of the Greek friends, Spiridion Blanke. The latter knew only modern Greek; my great-uncle only Attic Greek. Between them they produced what the French call a *mélange*, which is neither the one nor the other. Some of the words, and the form of the subjunctive, are to be found only in the contemporary language, whereas the construction and general intonation are those of the ancients.

In his Preface, Francesco Varè quotes and translates (this is a pity!—he would have done better to leave it in the original) a letter written by Voltaire to Goldoni. It is one of many proofs of the Frenchman's admiration for the Venetian. Another took the form of some verses, beginning *En tout pays on se pique* . . . which he sent to the Marchese Albergati in Bologna. Other admirers of Goldoni—composer, this time— put his comedies into music. Among these are Mozart, Haydn and Galuppi. The last named made an operetta out of Goldoni's *Arcadia in Brenta.*

But the attempt to translate the Venetian dialect into Attic Greek transcends them all!

*   *   *

In Goldoni's plays, Venice herself talks to us from behind a mask. We hear how the unfortunate *paterfamilias* (in *Barufe in Famigia*) despairs of ever getting his wife and his mother not to fight tooth and nail. In *Zente Refada*, the *nouveaux riches* are held up to ridicule, as they are in every successive generation. In *Mia fia*, a girl's failure to succeed on the stage brings sorrow to her parents. In *Serenissima*, the impoverished patrician, reduced to earn his bread as a humble clerk in the service of the municipality, retains the polished manners and the spiritual loftiness of noble forebears.

You will find Goldoni, in effigy, standing on a pedestal in Campo Santo Stefano, a few yards from the bridge of Rialto. Or you may meet his ghost strolling in the Merceria, a three-cornered hat cocked to one side over his wig; his tasselled cane tapping the ground as he walks. His plump legs are cased in woollen stockings; his coat is all buttons and loops On his mocking face is the same smile that lights up his plays.

Stop and talk to him, even if you have no Venetian. He speaks French, for in his old age he was at the Court of France. One of his best plays, *Le Bourru Bienfaisant*, was written on the occasion of the marriage of the heir to the throne, to an Austrian Princess, Marie Antoinette.

If you wish to ingratiate yourself, have a snuff-box handy; no need for the more costly and aromatic varieties of the herb. The famous play-wright is not proud. The ordinary varieties of rappee will do.

The characters in the *commedia dell'arte* are also there. If Goldoni is partly responsible for their demise, their ghosts still haunt their old home. Quite recently, on a night in August, I and my family looked on at a little play in the Campo Santa Margherita (one of the most spacious in Venice). They were giving the old comedy called *Le disgrazie di Pantalon, ovvero gli spaventi del Capitano Spaventa*. There was no theatre, no seats; only a raised and lighted stage, with rudimentary scenery— the traditional open space, with houses at both sides. Behind this platform, in deep shadow, stood an old Quattrocento building, called the Casa dei Verottari; once the headquarters of the Guild of the Tanners.

High in the skies, the moon was approaching fullness. A floodlit Madonna looked down—as if watching the play— from the tower of the Carmine. The tower itself was in darkness, so that she seemed to be suspended in the heavens. We could not see the Madonna's expression, but I feel sure that she smiled.

16

A PHANTOM CONFERENCE

IN the summer of 1954, an international gathering of over 100 poets was convoked in Venice (as once before in Salamanca), by the International Association of Poetry.

It may be true that a poet's mind is kindled by contact with another poet, as fire is kindled by contact with fire. But the announcement served to make me realize—as never before—that Pan was dead and, with him, all the gods of Hellas! The meeting became a subject for one of the Fourth Leaders in the London *Times*, opening with the comment: 'The lowest common denominator among poets is that they are queer fish; and queer fish cannot be thrown into one aquarium.'

The article went on to say that such congresses seldom include the best poets. They will be far away at home. They may even have forgotten to answer the invitation; they may even be writing poetry! This was not the reason that justified the absence of Mr. Ezra Pound. The American Government (as *The Times* leader mentioned) kept their country's most famous contemporary poet shut up in a lunatic asylum. A message of greetings was sent by his daughter, and the Conference dutifully sent a telegram back.

I have sat round green tables at too many international conferences to condole with any poet, who may be prevented from attending such meetings. Indeed, I'm not sure that a lunatic asylum does not offer a freer and wider range of outlook. The only conference, in my experience, that every artist might have enjoyed was held on the Lido of Venice, soon after the First World War. It concerned the Sud-Bahn and was presided over by the Marchese Imperiali, looking like a Roman Senator, robed in a bath-towel flung negligently over one shoulder, just as he had come out of the sea. I cannot imagine any of the great poets of the Past going into committee, drafting resolutions (in prose or rhyme), and feverishly seeking a 'formula' that should allow the delegates to get home by next Sunday.

As a matter of fact, I do remember a poet attending the Conference of San Remo, in April 1920. This was Robert Underwood Johnson, newly appointed American Ambassador to Rome. But his presence did not transform the meeting into a party capping rhymes, as in a game of '*bouts rimés*'. He listened to what was said by Lloyd George, Lord Curzon, Millerand and Scialoja, without intervening in the discussion.

He was considered a very eminent poet in his own country, though not like Ezra Pound. Two of his verses might apply to myself writing this book:

> And bended Age, whose rusted sickle lies
> In the scant harvest of remembered days.

*   *   *

There can be no reason why Shakespeare should not haunt the Rialto as much as Dante, or Goethe. There is more about Venice in Shakespeare's plays than in the *Divine Comedy*, or the *Italienische Reise*. Nor is it impossible that the creator of Shylock and of Portia knew the sea-town that, in their day, was a *Weltmarkt zwischen Morgen-und-Abendland*, the market-place of the Morning and Evening lands.

In the *Merchant of Venice* there is a brief scene that shows how the Author knew the difficulties for a stranger to find his way about.

GOBBO—Master, young gentleman, I pray you, which is the way to master Jew's?

LAUNCELOT—Turn up on your right hand, at the next turning, but at the very next turning of all, on your left; marry, at the very next turning, turn of no hand, but turn down indirectly to the Jew's house.

GOBBO—By God's sonties, 'twill be a hard way to hit!

It's no use asking the way of a Venetian. He (or she) will invariably point in the direction required and say: '*Vada sempre dritto* . . . meaning: Keep straight on. . . .' If there is one thing that you cannot do in the Venetian *calli* it is to keep straight on for more than ten yards or so. They are the narrowest crookedest, most inconsequent streets in the world.

*   *   *

If a Phantom Conference of poets were indeed to meet in Venice, it could not be 'covered' by the Press, at least not by living journalists. But perhaps the ghost of Salvatore Cortesi might attend, to represent the Associated Press, as he used to do in Italy, when alive.[1]

He might interview the major poets of the Past, and then—if he could get in touch with us—we would at last learn something definite about Shakespeare's personality.

Meanwhile, I will try myself, to call up some of the ghostly delegates.

*   *   *

It was from the Arsenal, not the *calli* or the canals, that Dante got one of his most effective similes for Canto XXI of the *Inferno*. He describes the seams of the ships being caulked with oakum and hot tar. To this tar he compares the boiling pitch in which the *Barattieri*—the barterers of office and of justice—are thrust by the Demons of the pit, armed with long forked prongs.

---

[1] See the present author's *Ghosts of the Spanish Steps*—(John Murray—London 1955), p. 137 *et sequitur*: 'The Cardinals and the Press'.

Quale nell'Arzanà de' Viniziani
Bolle l'inverno la tenace pece
A rimpalmar li lor legni non sani [1]

What does the *Divine Comedy* mean to most people out of Italy? What do Dante and Petrarch represent to the average foreigner? The 'man in the street' is familiar with Shakespeare's plays, for they are produced everywhere. But Dante's masterpiece is not easy reading, even for Italians, and is explained and commented on in the schools.

We know that Gladstone had a lifelong enthusiasm for it, and of the three parts he preferred the *Paradiso*. To quote John Morley's biography:

> Mr. Gladstone was always alive to the grandeur of Goethe's words, *Im Ganzen, Guten, Schönen, resolut zu leben*, but it was in Dante, active politician and thinker as well as poet, that he found the unity of thought and coherence of life, not only illuminated by a sublime imagination, but directly associated with theology, philosophy, politics, history, sentiment, duty. Here are all the elements and interests that lie about the roots of the life of a man and of the general civilization of the world.

Gladstone is far from being an 'average' man. One need not possess his compass of mind, the calibre of his intellectual qualities to meet Dante's ghost on Rialto, and recognize the slim figure in the long robe and the laurel crown on the falcon-hood. Come with me in the first hours of a summer day, when the clamour of the market-place is just beginning and boats laden with vegetables are unloading on the Riva del Vin. The stall-owners will be building cabbages into pyramids and wreathing the supports of their awnings with garlands of Spanish onions. The eating houses will be taking down the

---

[1] Like as in the Venetian's Arsenal
Boileth in winter the tenacious pitch
To tar again their un-seaworthy ships

Translation into blank verse by William Michael Rossetti (Macmillan, 1865).

shutters and preparing a breakfast of *sguassetto* for their earliest customers. Despite the bustle and the noise, some tired men lie stretched out on the ground *still* asleep. Near-by, opposite the church of San Giacomo, with its beautiful brick campanile, is the so-called Hunchback (*il Gobbo di Rialto*), patiently supporting the stand (made of marble, like himself), whence the Laws of the Republic were promulgated. And there, watching the scene as if seeking inspiration in it, stands the man whom Boccaccio describes as follows:

> This our poet was of middle stature; and, after he had arrived at mature age, he walked somewhat heavy. And his carriage was grave and courteous, clothed in most decorous garb, in that habit which was befitting his mature age. His visage was long; the nose aquiline, the eyes rather large than small, his hair and beard thick, black and crisp; [*N.B. The picture of him in the Bargello in Florence gives him brown hair*] the jaw large, and the under lip protruded beyond the upper; always his countenance was melancholy and thoughtful.
>
> It happened one day in Verona, the fame of his works being already noised everywhere, and chiefly of that part of his Comedy which he entitles Hell, and he being known by many men and women, he passing before a door whereat several women were sitting, one of them in an undertone, but still well heard by him and such as were with him, said to the other women: 'See ye him who goes through hell, and returns when he lists, and brings up hither news of those who are down there?' Whereto one of them replied in her simplicity: 'Of a truth, thou must say true. Seest not how he has his beard shrivelled up and his complexion brown, through the heat and the smoke which are there below?' Which words hearing said behind him, and knowing that they came of the pure credence in the women, he, pleased and as it were content that they should be in such belief, somewhat smiling, passed on.

It could never have happened to Dante—as it happened to Shakespeare—to give rise to arguments intended to attribute the authorship of his works to someone else. Shakespeare's art is objective to such an extent that he deprives himself of his

personal identity, and disappears behind his own creations:
Falstaff and Shylock; Caesar and Othello; Juliet and Cleopatra;
Perdita and Lady Macbeth. At court and in the cottage, with
real men or with fairies, he is equally at home. No other poet
has described, as he has, the whole of the human race, casting
himself into the heart and soul of every character whom he
brings upon the stage. But he appears to have been forbidden
by Heaven to come forward to the footlights, after the final
curtain, to receive the applause that the audience would
offer to the author, as well as to the actors.

Dante's art is subjective, and his greatest poem is an autobiography, even if it speaks of a world-to-come, a world
beyond our ken. Mortal problems follow him through immortality. The spirits of the damned forget their torments,
when his voice reaches them, speaking the Tuscan dialect.
Florentines ask him the news of political factions in their
native town. These are more real to them than the fire that is
never quenched, where the Worm dieth not.

The poet's personality is always before the reader's eyes.
We know that Dante loved Beatrice. Her spirit, impersonating
Faith, leads him upwards, like the *ewig Weibliche* of Goethe,
to the very presence of God.[1]

*   *   *

In the galaxy of poet-ghosts, who would feel quite at home on
Rialto, there is another figure in a long robe, wearing a hood
and laurel-crown: the ghost of Petrarch. He died at Arquà in

[1] See in the present author's *Laughing Diplomat* (John Murray, London
1938), p. 208.

The national genius of Italy tends to concentrate, to unify. Thus, in
religion, they create the Papacy. And you will discover the same characteristic
in literature, if you compare the *Divine Comedy* to the plays of Shakespeare.
On the one side, a single organic conception, that unites Hell and Purgatory
and Paradise in the poet's vision. On the other hand, as many conceptions
and as varied as are the characters in Shakespeare's plays.

the Euganean Hills, and left his library to the Venetian Republic. That was the first library of the Renaissance, and Petrarch the first of the Humanists. He revived classical learning at the close of the Middle Ages; a task full of difficulties and disappointments, as when we find him poring over a Homer that he could not read, knowing no Greek. He regarded the authors of antiquity as depositaries of a tradition only second in importance to the Holy Scriptures and revelation. For him, there was no schism between Rome and Galilee.

He bequeathed to his many imitators some masterpieces of lyrical art, unrivalled for perfection in workmanship. But this was not the greatest of his achievements. He opened out for Europe a new sphere of mental activity. The modern world owes more to Petrarch than, perhaps, it is aware of. In the world he lived in, he had the merit of being the first poet of love—his love for Laura—to shake off the shackles of allegory and mysticism. His *Canzoniere* is one long melody—on the subject of a beautiful woman—poured from the poet's soul.

This is all very well. But I cannot forget Mark Twain's comment on the world-famous love of Petrarch for Laura. He said: 'The person I'm sorry for is Mr. Laura!'

*   *   *

In an important international congress, on world affairs, there are the delegates of the Great Powers, and those of the little ones. The latter are often the more skilful diplomats, but their national prestige is lower. The third Marquis of Salisbury, representing Great Britain at the Congress of Berlin in June 1878, wrote home: 'The heat is excessive. In Potsdam there are mosquitoes. Here, the minor powers. I don't know which are worse.'

In the Phantom Conference we are speaking of, the minor poets would doubtless represent the mosquitoes. They form a contingent little known outside a very limited area. One of these was Genero (I have forgotten his Christian name), who occupied a small apartment on the Bacino Orseolo, just a few yards from the Piazza. I seem to remember that he wrote quite good verses, though not a poet by profession; only because his demon urged him to express himself in verse. He was a chiropodist, indeed the only one in Venice. His spectre might attend the Phantom Conference in a double capacity.

Or don't ghosts have corns?

*   *   *

Some people who are not so by temperament become poets in Venice.

Of these, one was Friedrich Wilhelm Nietzsche. He is best known (at least out of Germany) as the creator of the 'Superman', who gives unbridled freedom to the struggle for existence. Nietzsche's mind became unhinged, when he was forty years old, and he died, in 1900, in an asylum. He had, in his heart, a very tender spot for Venice. It may be that he found there his Lethe, and the blessings of Oblivion.

I found a little poem of his, when reading Edward Jaime's *Kleine Geschichte Venedigs*. It is a *Gondollieder*, like the famous barcarolle in the *Tales of Hoffmann*. Not perhaps a very good poem, for it is written '*im beginne der Umnachtung*' when the darkness of night was already closing on the mind of this philosopher of revolt against the whole civilized environment in which he was brought up.

Nietzsche had evidently made friends with a real gondolier, and I wonder if he could have known old Luigi Zatta, who died in 1905, at the age of seventy-two?

I myself remember Zatta well and was impressed by all the honours he had won, in the annual regattas, as well as by the fact that Queen Margherita once spoke to me about him. It appears that old King Umberto had talked with Zatta, who

CORTINA D'AMPEZZO IN 1894 (See p. 43)

POPE PIUS X *(See p. 158)*

had declared that it was better to be a gondolier than a king, even though the *felze* (or cover) of his own gondola was getting old and would not last another winter.

To get back to Nietzsche: among the aphorisms and epigrams by which he best expressed himself, I find, in *Ecce Homo*, the following: 'If I search for another word for Music, I find always and only Venice.'

This does not appear self-evident to most people, and I was puzzled, at first, by so much emphasis. But it is true that Venice was, for some time (and before Nietzsche's time) a centre for classical German music, especially choral music. Händel, Glück, even Mozart, sought inspiration in Venice. Probably there was a certain chivalrous affectation in the homage paid by some German musicians to the city of the lagoons. They even spoke of Vienna as the *Tochter-Stadt*.

* * *

I was a fervent admirer of Alfred de Musset, in my youth, and I naturally include him in the list of possible delegates to the Phantom Conference. But in doing so I regret having to couple his name with that of Armandine Dudevant, whose *nom de guerre* was George Sand. This masculine pseudonym and the fact that she was one of the first women to wear trousers takes away from the attraction of the love-affair. Elizabeth Browning wrote of her:

> True genius, but true woman! dost deny
> The woman's nature with a manly scorn,

Very true, no doubt. But, this being the case, I wish she did not figure, in the history of literature, as the woman in André Maurois' classic *Les Amants de Venise*, not to mention the more recent biography, called *Lelia*, out of a character in one of her own books.

De Musset must have been attractive in his youth, full of

grace and assurance, and rather dandified. In this, as in other things, he imitated Byron, for whom he had an unstinted admiration. His critics accused him of dealing out 'du Byron' by the kilo!

Before starting for Venice with him, George Sand had called on de Musset's mother and obtained her reluctant consent to the poet's accompanying her to Italy. The experience was supposed to be good for such a brilliant young man. They started at the beginning of winter, but in April of the following year, Alfred reappeared in Paris, in broken health and in the deepest depression. He had fallen ill in Venice, with symptoms of brain fever, and George had nursed him with great tenderness (he was occupying No. 15 in the so-called Gallery of the Hotel Danieli). At the same time, she was making love to the young Italian doctor, Pagello, who attended the poet in his sickness.

Some flashes of humour have illumined the story, such as Swinburne's: 'Alfred was a terrible flirt, and George did not behave as a perfect gentleman.' But neither pathos nor humour can alter an impression that there was something unpleasant about the whole episode.

De Musset's *Confession d'un Enfant du Siècle* is not an autobiography, but a striking study of moral pathology. Yet he can be wholesome, and gay and tender, as in his play *A quoi rêvent les Jeunes Filles,* or when he writes of Venice.

*   *   *

I can claim to have known one real poet, whose ghost might attend a Phantom Conference in Venice: Gabriele d'Annunzio. We saw a lot of each other in the days of my youth, but mostly in Rome. When I came back to Europe from China, in January 1920, d'Annunzio was in the middle of the Fiume escapade and busy defying the Allies (including the Italian Government); also abusing President Wilson, who was his special *bête noire*. I was surprised to find so many people, even among Americans, who agreed with him in this.

On one of the few occasions when I met d'Annunzio in Venice, we went together into the Basilica of St. Mark's. He remarked on the mosaics that sheath the whole interior, except where coloured figures, in crowded imagery, tell the story of the Redemption. Each of the tiny *tesselae* is made of two small fragments of glass, holding between them a piece of gold leaf. Thus—as my companion pointed out—the whole of St. Mark's is sheeted in gold. The Zeno chapel is vaulted with cupolas that are starred in gold. The famous Pala d'Oro, behind the principal altar, is a screen of solid gold.

D'Annunzio enthused over all this till I protested: 'Bother you and your gold, Gabriele! If you had been a suitor for the hand of Portia, you would have been like the Duke of Morocco and chosen the golden casket!'

He answered: 'Bassanio is welcome to the leaden one and to the lady! I never could stand *les femmes savantes*.'

And he murmured, half under his breath, one of his own verses: '*Date a me l'oro, come a Benvenuto*' (Give *me* gold, as to Benvenuto').

It is perhaps true that there can hardly be too much gold, too much jewelled magnificence, in so old a Basilica. The shadowy aisles are lit only by a ray or two from a distant casement and by the feeble light of hanging lamps, reflected on polished slabs of alabaster.

Gabriele's passion for magnificence came out continually in his novels and in some of his plays, but he was equally at home in the peasant's cottage—as in *La Figlia di Jorio*—or among the desolation of dead cities—as in *La Città Morta*.

To this day, I don't know how to judge Gabriele as a man and as an artist.

Giuseppe Chiarini, who first drew the attention of the public to the young poet, later on showed a marked diffidence to a writer who might corrupt the morals of youth. (Chiarini was once Head of the school I attended as a boy.) There was never any danger of his corrupting mine! I was fascinated, but not attracted; often repelled. The flow and forcefulness of his words impressed me, not his philosophy. Some of his earlier works, tales of his boyhood, *Le Novelle della Pescara*, filled me with horror.

But Chiarini was quite right in fearing the influence that Gabriele might exercise over simple minds, even if they could understand very little of what he wrote and said. Apart from the question of corrupting their morals, it is true that Gabriele's writings and his speeches appealed to people who could not be expected to follow his reasoning. Long after his day was over, my eldest daughter (not a literary person) pored over the apotheosis of the sea in his epic *La Nave*, much as, a few years before, she had been entranced by maroons and schooners and Pieces of Eight in *Treasure Island*. I was told that his followers to Fiume—rough soldiers and sailors—listened open-mouthed to his harangues.

Most poets, at one time or another, cross the Rubicon between Thought and Action. Gabriele did so with Dionysiac frenzy! Among aviators, in the first world war, he proved himself the bravest of the brave. Aeroplanes being what they were then, his flight over Vienna, to drop leaflets, was a foolhardy deed, if only for the length of enemy territory he had to traverse. Once, in an accident on landing, he got thrown against the plane's machine-gun, and lost an eye. But he defied the doctor's warning that, unless he was careful to avoid the sunlight, he might lose the other eye as well.

So much vigour and strength seemed incompatible with the refinements of a polished æstheticism. But, like most outstanding characters, he was full of contradictions.

It was typical of Gabriele's mentality that he should have shown a marked sympathy and admiration for the 'mad' King Ludwig II of Bavaria. He almost appeared to agree with Verlaine that Ludwig was *le seul roi du siècle*! Nine years after the death of the King, Gabriele spoke of him as having been 'childish and sublime'. In the romance *Le Vergini delle Rocce,* he wrote: 'This Wittelsbach attracts me because of his pride and his sadness.' The King's devotion, to Wagner, amounting to idolatry, also attracted him, for he shared it.

The title of one of Gabriele's last works, *Forse che si, forse che no,* is taken from the motto written and rewritten on the ceiling-cornice of the Gonzaga Palace in Mantua, where Isabella d'Este reigned. The heavy, scent-laden atmosphere of the novel is almost unbreathable. Among the great ladies of the fifteenth and sixteenth centuries, Isabella, most strikingly personified the spirit of the Renaissance. In his *Italian Fantasies,* Israel Zangwill criticizes Gabriele's book in a chapter called 'Denunciation of d'Annunzio'. Zangwill objects to the 'materialization' of Isabella d'Este, for Gabriele sees her only as a 'Magnificent One', reigning in a palace of 180 rooms, where there was even a miniature apartment for the Court Jesters, the dwarfs, and where Isabella's brother-in-law, Lodovico il Moro, visited her with a suite of a thousand persons. Gabrielle—so Zangwill complains—revels in all the grandeur and the gold. He sees her less as the Princess that Titian painted (the portrait is now in Vienna), than as a great courtesan, surrounded by pages and poets and buffoons, painters and broiderers, goldsmiths and engravers. *Vanitas vanitatum, omnia vanitas!*

Something of all this vanity can be found, not only in the pages of *Forse che si, forse che no,* but also in Gabriele's former romance, *Fuoco.* The *Encyclopaedia Britannica,* mentioning this book in an article on Gabriele, says that it contains the most ardent glorification of a city, existing in any language. The city is Venice.

In *Fuoco,* Gabriele portrays himself under the name of Stelio Effrena, a poet musician, like Wagner, writing the libretti for his own operas. These operas have wonderful Preludes, full of Italian fire, German thunder and the melancholy of the

Slavs. Wagner figures in the book, and the panegyric is as much for the real musician as for the imaginary one. A *leit-motif* of Destiny runs through both their lives.

The heroine, sometimes called 'la Fornarina' and sometimes Perdita, is a great actress: in real life, Eleonora Duse. The author hardly does her justice and makes her out more neurotic than she really was. Even when writing of the woman he loves, Gabriele is thinking all the time of himself. But there are some pages about Perdita's feelings, when about to start on a tour, to act in America, which are very fine. He describes the susceptibilities of the woman who lives for her art and suffers from the noisy publicity that surrounds her in a great town, where her name stares at her from every wall, pasted over with notices of her performances.

Although Gabriele's prose made me feel as if I were being fed exclusively on caviare and plum-pudding (too rich a diet for my simple taste), I had to admit that he knew how to give expression, not only to sensual pleasures and the extravagance of a voluptuary, but also to the philosophy of asceticism. He could portray St. Francis of Assisi.

Perhaps this is because St. Francis was a poet. Did he not name the fire 'brother', and water 'sister', and in his sermon to the fishes remind them that they alone were saved in the flood? And he sang with Sister Grasshopper for eighty days. To him the world was small because so many relatives could be found in it. In the loneliest star that the great telescope of Palomar can reveal to us, he would have beheld only the features of a new friend.

In Gabriele's books, St. Francis appears often. The poet, though not a believer, was a mystic. He could rhapsodize over the jewelled reliquaries in the Treasury of St. Mark's, and on the silence and desolation of that tiny islet, beyond Murano, where stand the modest church and monastery, named San Francesco del Deserto.

He went there one morning in early spring, with the Duse.

Women are not allowed to enter the cloister, so she waited for him in the gondola, listening to the larks that filled the air with their song. A blue haze marked the outline of the Euganean Hills.

Under the wooden roof of a little columned portico hung the empty nests of swallows that later would return. Gabriele had disappeared together with a young friar. It was very silent and remote, on the outer bulwarks of the lagoon. The sun shone on the water and down to the submerged seaweed, brown with golden lights on it, like the century-old mosaics in St. Mark's. The two gondoliers sat on the bank, resting before the long row home. Behind them, a row of young cypresses pierced the sky, and two older trees that had been struck by lightning, lifted their mutilated trunks into the blue.

After a while, Gabriele came back with a sprig of blossom in his hand, which he had picked from a flowering almond-tree. The young friar also brought an offering to the lady in the gondola, perhaps to console her for not having been allowed in. It was a little nosegay of fragrant thyme.

She asked him if the Saint would not be distressed at his orchard being despoiled. The little friar answered: 'To tell the truth, this gentleman had plucked the branch of blossom before I could stop him, but it does not matter. The tree is rich.'

Smiling at the friar's simplicity, the great actress said she would recite to him, the *Laudi* of St. Francis; his 'Praises of the Creatures'. And in that golden voice of hers, she began:

'Praise be the Lord for our own Mother Earth, who feeds and governs us, and gives us varied fruits and grasses. . . .'

And went on till the end:

'Praise be the Lord for our own sister Death—*per nostra corporal sorella Morte!*'

Late that afternoon, when the lovers stepped out of their gondola on the Fondamenta Sanudo, they were met with the sad news:

'Richard Wagner is dead!'

157

17

THE SAINT

JOAN: O God that madest this beautiful earth; when will
it be ready to receive Thy saints?

BERNARD SHAW—*St. Joan*—end

IT is not everybody who can boast of having taken coffee with
a saint. I mean a real saint, subsequently canonized in the
church calendar and with a saint's-day to his name.

I am speaking of Giuseppe Sarto, at one time Patriarch of
Venice. In the year 1903, he became Pope, with the name of
Pius X.

A Venetian friend in Rome had asked me to procure him a
small piece of information of an ecclesiastical nature, so I went
to the Patriarch's *palazzo*, next door to the Basilica of St.
Mark's, not knowing whom I might find. It was with no little
astonishment that on ringing a bell, I found myself facing
Cardinal Sarto himself, who had opened the door to me. He
was holding a large feather fan in his right hand: one of those
fans, with a wooden handle, that Italian cooks use (or used to
use) to stimulate the embers in the kitchen stove. He remarked
casually that he was making himself a cup of coffee, and
suggested my having one too.

He did not know me, but that was his way: always to offer
something, always to practise what St. Paul said to the
Elders of Ephesus, that it is more blessed to give than to
receive. We knew in Venice that our Patriarch received his
Mensa (his ecclesiastical stipend) every three months, but those
moneys never lasted him more than a few weeks, at the end

of which he was almost destitute, having given everything away in charities. In this way, he remained always a suitor (like St. Francis) of Lady Poverty. He wore his predecessor's robes, in order not to buy new ones, and often pawned his watch, to give the money to some person in trouble. In fact he was always pawning something. Once a rich lady in Padua gave him a fine ring, to replace the very modest pastoral ring he was wearing. He kept the ring, but replaced the valuable stone with a cheap bit of glass, to the horrified amazement of the donor, who noticed the change!

We talked together in the Venetian dialect (which I don't speak very well), and he gave me the information I wanted. It was only when I was about to leave that it occurred to him to ask who I was. When I mentioned my name, he looked puzzled and said: 'But you don't live in Venice, now, do you?'

I told him that I was pursuing my studies in Rome. He said something about the greatness of Rome, but added: 'It is pleasanter here, *dalle parti nostre.*' (In our own part of the country.)

I remembered this remark of his, when I heard of his election by the Conclave of Cardinals, to be Supreme Pontiff. And I heard afterwards that, as soon as this appeared likely (after the Austrian Emperor's veto, excluding Cardinal Rampolla), he begged the other cardinals not to choose him. But they persisted, and he was practically forced to accept, which he did with tears in his eyes. He compared his new task to Calvary and spoke of the Cross that he must bear. And all this without a shred of affectation, in all sincerity and misgiving. Had he not promised his beloved Venetians that he would come back to them 'alive or dead', and hadn't he, when starting off, taken a return ticket?

He was delighted, soon after his arrival for the Conclave, when a French cardinal assured him that he could not aspire to the Papal Tiara (he was not *papabile*) because he spoke no French, but only Latin.

His predecessor, Leo XIII, of the Pecci family, was an

aristocrat and a man of the world, with a biting wit and a
caustic tongue. The stories told about him (and they were
many) were very different from those that centred round
Giuseppe Sarto.[1]

Pius X was comfortably stout and had the broad, rugged
features of a peasant. His humour was homely and genial,
never unkind.

A weak man can never become a saint, and Pius X was
both a strong man and a strong Pope. In the matter of discipline he unflinchingly vindicated the Church's right to depose
delinquent bishops, even though this meant breaking off
diplomatic relations with France.

Sometimes, I try to recapture my feelings of the time when
we had coffee together. But all I can remember is the exquisite
innocence in those tired, kind brown eyes.

I am not perhaps the best person to draw a comparison
(if only a physical one) between the two Popes who succeeded
one another, when I was still a young man. Yet I would like
to bring out in greater relief, the figure of Pius X.

Perhaps I can do so with the help of two authors, whose
command of the English language is certainly greater than
mine, though their style is pure Ottocento. The first is an
account taken from Mrs. Humphry Ward's *Eleanor*. The
author describes Pope Leo XIII during a great ceremony in St.
Peter's, under the dome of Michelangelo. A young American
girl is brought, for the first time in her life, into contact with
the Roman Catholic Church, and sees the Pope in his chair,
la Sedia Gestatoria, carried through the crowd to the High Altar:

[1] Let me give an example, in a footnote, if not in the text.

Pope Leo XIII was thin to the point of emaciation, with a huge mouth
and prominent ears. Not an easy subject for a portrait-painter. However a
Spanish painter did a portrait of him and was so pleased with his own work
that he asked the Pontiff to write a verse from the Bible underneath his
own likeness. The Pope did not like the idea, but in the end he consented.
He took the paint brush that was handed to him and wrote on the canvas:
'Be not afraid. It is I!'

There—there he is—the old man! Caught in a great shaft of sunlight striking from south to north, across the church, the Pope
emerges. The white figure, high above the crowd, sways from side
to side; the hand upraised gives the benediction. Fragile, spiritual
as is the apparition, the sunbeam refines, subtilizes it still more.
It hovers like a dream above the vast multitudes—surely no living
man!—but thought, history, faith, taking shape; the passion of
many hearts revealed. . . .

This is St. Peter's; there is the dome of Michelangelo; and
here, advancing towards her amid the red of the cardinals, the
clatter of the guards, the tossing of the flabellae, as though looking
at her alone—the two waxen fingers raised for her alone—is the
white-robed triple-crowned Pope! . . . vaguely she wonders that
the old man keeps his balance, as he clings with one frail hand to
the arm of the chair, rises incessantly—and blesses with the
other. She catches the very look and meaning of the eyes—the
sharp long line of the closed and toothless jaw. Spirit and spectre;
embodying the Past, bearing the clue to the Future. . . .

. . . The mass is over, a temporary platform has been erected
between the Confession and the nave. The Pope has been placed
upon it, and is about to chant the Apostolic Benediction. . . .
The red Cardinal holding the service-book, the groups of guards,
clergy and high officials, every detail of the Pope's gorgeous dress,
nay every line of the wrinkled face, and fleshless hands, Lucy's
eyes command them all. The quavering voice rises into the sudden
silence of St. Peter's. Fifty thousand people hush every movement;
strain their ears to listen.

Ah! How weak it is! Surely the effort is too great for a frame so
enfeebled, so ancient. It should not have been exacted—allowed.
Lucy's ears listen painfully for the inevitable break. But no!—
The Pope draws a long sigh—the sigh of weakness ('Ah! poveretto!'
says a woman close to Lucy, in a transport of pity);—then once
more attempts the chant—sighs again—and sings. Lucy's face
softens and glows; her eyes fill with tears. Nothing more touching,
more triumphant, than this weakness and this perseverance.
Fragile indomitable face, beneath the Papal crown! Under the
eyes of fifty thousand people, the Pope sighs like a child, because
he is weak and old, and the burden of his office is great; but in

sighing, keeps a perfect simplicity, dignity, courage. Not a trace of stoical concealment; but also not a trace of flinching. He sings to the end, and St. Peter's listens in a tender hush.

*　　　*　　　*

And now for Leo's successor: the Pope who was no aristocrat, no politician, but by his own nature a 'man of God', and the only Pope to be canonized during many centuries. The two Pontiffs, so unlike in character, follow one another in the long series of bishops who form an unbroken line between St. Peter and Linus (mentioned by St. Paul in his last letter to Timothy), handing on the same traditions, making the same claims.

It happened that, soon after Giuseppe Sarto became Pope Pius X (and was thus cut off, for his lifetime, from his beloved Venice), a young American author came to Rome, by name Booth Tarkington, who had just established his reputation on both sides of the Atlantic, by a book called *Monsieur Beaucaire* (subsequently dramatized).

Soon after the election of Pius X, in the winter of 1903-4, Booth Tarkington was present at a ceremony in the Cortile di San Damaso. This is one of the principal courtyards in the Vatican, just behind St. Peter's. The Pope was to receive and speak to a group of young girls. Many people of all sorts were invited to assist. Tarkington wrote an account of this 'Vatican Sermon', which was published in *Harper's Magazine* for June 1904.

The following is a brief resumé of that article.

Under the gay sky of a winter Sunday, nearly all the cabs in Rome were scurrying towards St. Peter's. There was one long parade of them returning along the Tiber embankment, having discharged their loads. The stream of people went through the gate to emerge upon a great court, which is enclosed partly by the palace, partly by a large open gallery.

Opposite the gallery stood a very large platform, higher than the heads of the spectators. It was hung with red velvet and gold. A dais supported the papal throne. Upon each side of the throne stood rigidly a tall steel-helmeted Swiss Guard in his brilliant stripes, long pike in hand.

The Society of the Daughters of Mary entered in procession, girls in white dresses with long veils; they took places nearest the platform, for it was to them, particularly, that the Pope would speak.

The people were waiting happily. There were many country people and many poor. Florentines, Neapolitans, soft-spoken Venetians and a few dark Sicilians were there with the Roman crowd. There were Germans, Frenchmen, and a hundred or so Americans and English, the former eagerly interested and looking so, the latter the same but not looking so.

Among the former were two young people whose nationality was marked, partly by their keen, humorous, expectant eyes; somewhat, too, by the fashion of their clothes. They were a Chicago bride and groom on their wedding journey. She kept her slim grey glove tucked through his arm, and they both showed openly that the coming spectacle might be beautiful, but was necessarily remote: arranged for the two to look at as a momentary diversion from their permanent vocation of looking at each other.

A bell within the palace tinkled. With a wide flash of brass and silver, the instruments rose simultaneously to the mouths of the musicians, and the papal anthem leaped out jubilantly from the horns. Another bell, and into the anthem there broke a deep and splendid roll of drums. These were the heralds of the coming of the presence. They rolled out their long salute, while a dozen stately and glittering officers filed slowly out upon the platform and ranged themselves in a semicircle, flanking each side of the dais. They were followed by as many ecclesiastics in purple and red; and now the clamour of the crowd grew into an uproar, then suddenly rose to thunder as there appeared a single figure, all in magnificent white, amidst the mass of red and gold and purple. The officers and ecclesiastics knelt as the Pope passed to his throne; and to the young Americans, who had, all at once, found inexplicable tears in their eye, it seemed quite natural that those dignitaries should kneel.

For Pius X had the effect of pathos; or perhaps it was the transparent and touching quality of simple goodness that was in his face. Many a town in the United States has been blessed with a citizen of this type; a strong and kindly 'Uncle Billy Jackson', an old fellow carrying the radiance of a life spent in good works, the service of those in need; one whose hale greeting in the street made the recipient better and gayer all day; that rare thing, a genial philanthropist, whose heart and hand and scanty store were not for the orphan alone, not for the unhighly educated alone, but for all who lacked, or sinned, or mourned; for the grieving child, the lame dog, the drunkard, for the stranger fallen sick.

Seeing him, one understood well his sorrow in the great trust which he had not sought, his homesickness for the beloved Venice he would never see again!

There was something about him too, which made the little bride lean closer to her young husband, as she said, huskily: 'He seems so like the good bishop in *Les Misérables*. I know he would have given Jean Valjean the stolen silver!'

The Pope stood in front of the throne, smiling a little, and looking down upon his people; for his they were from the moment they saw him. In all that happy and enthusiastic crowd, it is probable that no one, Roman or stranger, lacked the feeling that the Pope liked him and would have been glad to know him in a friendly, easy way. There was not a touch of the politician. The man's doctrine was in the beauty of the expression of his fine, rugged peasant face. It was a return to Christianity.

Pius X was of good height, strongly made, even stout, and had a fine grace of carriage; his dignity as great as his position, but utterly without haughtiness or pomposity, or pride of office. He had none of the 'magnetism' of the 'popular preacher', actor or orator; nevertheless he was remarkably magnetic; it was the magnetism of unmistakable goodness and good-will to all the world.

The full, joyful voices of the novices rose in the open air over the pulsing instruments. It was as if the young girls had, all at once, bloomed gloriously into music. The people listened intently; yet no one looked at the singers; rarely an eye wandered even for a moment from the Pope.

'It is like music set not to words,' whispered the little bride, 'but to a face.'

The Pope came forward and stood, near the edge of the platform, to speak to the Daughters of Mary—and to all the people. Silence fell instantly; there was only the faint, multitudinous rustle as everyone leaned forward a little, intent to listen.

His voice, mellow, clear and resonant, yet gentle, had in it the quality of lofty and practical goodness that was in his face. It was what might have been called a 'brave' voice. A man with that kind of voice would not be afraid of anything that might happen to himself only. But more than these things, it carried the benediction that exhaled from the spirit of Pius X, to all the world, all the time.

While he was speaking, the great clock, high over his head, belled out the hour, four. So intent were the people not to lose a syllable, that a thousand unconscious whispers reproved each solemn stroke, saying 'Sh!' to the bell.

Quite silently and without so much as the sound of a foot scuffling the pavement, the crowd had drawn forward and closer, until at last they formed a dense press; so that when the Pope raised his arms for the benediction and the people knelt to receive his blessing, the whole mass surged back, like a receding wave.

The Chicagoans were expecting the congregation to file out in decorous silence after the benediction, and they were infinitely surprised, and delighted as well, when the people, rising, began to cheer with all their hearts. The enthusiasm which had greeted the coming of the Pope, burst out many times, intensified by the silence which had pent it up; and it was the greater because the feeling for the man had grown deeper every second. His coming had thrilled the people; at first sight they had liked him; now they loved him.

Pius X smiled down upon it all from the red throne. One of his attendants had brought him a beautiful red hat and a long red coat, for now the western hills were casting their cold shadows over the city.

The little bride, awed and full of many thoughts, walked lingeringly, her head over her shoulder, looking back wistfully.

'There's something so sad about him,' she said, 'something so sad and so kind!'

They reached the arch, and she stopped for a last look at the picture they would never see again. The silver-shot blue of the late afternoon sky bent in like a canopy over the brown palace walls; the brilliant semicircle of officers, helmeted guards, and prelates glittered about the red throne, whereon sat the central figure of all the world—so it seemed at that moment—the good and simple-hearted old man in his gorgeous white and red, his kindly eyes beaming good-will from under the splendid hat.

'Ah, isn't he wonderful!' said the little bride; and then, in her girlish tenderness and admiration, she found the inadequate and incongruous word that was luminous with the human meaning the Pope of Rome had for her: 'Oh, isn't he a *dear!*'

* * *

Pope Pius X is mentioned in another book of mine,[1] when I describe the visit paid him, in 1905, by Pierpont Morgan. The journalist, Salvatore Cortesi, acted as interpreter. His job was not an easy one, as both Pope and financier were afflicted, during the meeting, with an incredible nervousness. Both were

[1] *Twilight of the Kings* (John Murray, London 1948).

so shy and embarrassed that neither knew how to begin a conversation. Cortesi had to take the initiative and put them at their ease (a strange situation, and not uninteresting from the point of view of a psychologist). What was the cause of such unusual timidity in two men—both of them were 'men of the world'—neither of whom was habitually shy with strangers?

Once the ice had been broken, conversation became normal, and the two potentates—in such different spheres—even asked each other personal questions and compared their respective ages.

Cortesi had known Giuseppe Sarto when he was Patriarch of Venice, and by reason of this old acquaintance, was on friendly terms with the Pope, and was granted frequent private audiences. On one of these occasions, the Holy Father said to him:

'By the way, I have received a letter from an American surety company asking for information about you. But why should they apply to me?'

Cortesi had to confess that he had been having a little joke with the company. The Associated Press required that all chiefs of their foreign offices who handled funds should give a bond. These bonds were provided by a surety company, which required that each applicant should give two references as to his character and respectability. When Cortesi was asked to obtain a bond, the New York office sent him a form to fill in, giving the names and addresses of two people, well known in the U.S.A., who could vouch for him. He had filled in the blank as follows:

NAME	OCCUPATION	ADDRESS
Giuseppe Sarto	Pope	Vatican Palace, Rome (Italy)
Victor Emmanuel of Savoy	King	Quirinal Palace, Rome (Italy)

Cortesi had forgotten all about it till the Pope reminded him of it by showing him the letter from the insurance company. Pius X was delighted. He always enjoyed a joke. And he assured Cortesi that he would give him a good character.

There are books about Pius X (such as *San Pio X*, by San Gal, published in Padua, in 1954), describing his stand against Modernism, his reform of sacred music; his relations with the French Government and the French people; the great works of charity which crowned all the personal charities of his daily life. But it is by the little familiar stories that he is remembered in Venice, where the common people spoke of him sometimes as 'our Patriarch', and sometimes simply as 'Bepi' (short for Giuseppe) a name he shared with my Aunt Caterina's cat.

There is the story of the little nun who begged him to send her a pair of his stockings, to cure the rheumatism in her legs. He sent her an old pair, as requested. And she wore them for a time, after which she declared that she was perfectly cured.

'That is odd,' said the Pope. 'I wore those stockings longer than she did. They never did *my* rheumatism any good!'

A Roman lady, whom he knew well, was received in private audience. The Pope took the opportunity of asking her about the new-fangled dances that were invading our ballrooms and which some people disapproved of.

What the lady answered I don't know, but the Pope asked her why such dances should be imported from overseas, when there were many old Italian dances that might still delight young people, out for fun.

'Such as?' the lady enquired.

'Such as the *furlana*, they dance in Venetia.'

'But we don't know it!'

'Well, perhaps I could show you the steps. . . .'

And the dear old man danced, as best he could, to show what the *furlana* was like.

*   *   *

Pius X died of a broken heart, a few days after the outbreak of the First World War. He had seen it coming long before any statesman, by a kind of psychic intuition that had nothing to do with political foresight or inside knowledge. There are reliable witnesses to this prescience. One was the Brazilian ambassador in Rome, who was recalled in 1913.

'You are fortunate in going home,' said the Pope to him, 'where you will be far from the seat of the war.' The ambassador thought he meant the war in the Balkans. Only later did he realize it was not so.

One of the last decisions taken by him was his refusal to accede to a request from the Emperor Franz Josef to bless the Austrian army. The Pope answered: 'I bless peace, not war.'

On the sarcophagus where his body first lay, in the crypt of St. Peter's, were engraved the words *Pauper sed dives*. He was born poor, lived poor and died poor. The eldest son of ten children, his father had been a *cursore* (a sort of errand boy and handyman) for the municipality of Riese, with a pay of fifty centimes a day (about three dollars monthly). His mother was the village seamstress.

When he died, he had three sisters living. In his will, he asked that the Holy See might give them an allowance of 300 lire a month.

During the process of canonization, many miracles were attributed to him and admitted as authentic by the Tribunal that inquires into such matters. Apart from this, we all knew of cases that the doctors had given up as hopeless, but which he declared not to be so. And he was always right.

One was the case of the old Sacristan of St. Mark's, whose daughter-in-law was sick unto death. Three doctors declared that she had not much longer to live. The Patriarch consented to say a Mass for her. When this was over, he took the old Sacristan home with him and gave him coffee. The Sacristan offered the 'charity money' owing for the Mass. But the Patriarch said: 'No. Don't give it to me. Buy something for your daughter-in-law.'

'But she is dying!'

'No. She won't die. She will get well.'

And so she did.

18

THE BEAUTIES

NICCOLO' TRON DOGE LXVIII—nell'anno 1471

Era questo Senatore di 74 anni quando fu eletto Principe, nel cui tempo Caterina Cornaro si diede in moglie a Jacopo Re di Cipro, e dovendosi Ella partire, si fecero nella Città molte feste, e il Doge fu a riceverla col Bucintoro a San Polo, e con Real pompa l' accompagnò fino al Lido, dove sali sulle Galee, che la condussero in Cipro.

Cronaca Veneta Sacra e Profana della Città di Venezia—1793[1]

ACCORDING to Molmenti, the famous 'Titian bronze' of the ladies' hair was due more to washes and to exposure to the sun, than to a natural colouring indigenous to Venetian women.

To take three ladies, renowed in different times for their beauty: Caterina Cornaro, Marina Benzon and Annina Morosini—none of them had any Titian bronze in their hair. The first two were fair-haired. Annina Morosini had black hair (at least to begin with) and green eyes.

Caterina Cornaro (1454-1510), whose portrait by Titian hangs in the Uffizi Gallery in Florence, came of an ancient

---

[1] Translation—NICCOLO' TRON DOGE number LXVIII in the year 1471.

This Senator was seventy-four years old when he was elected Prince, in which time Caterina Cornaro was given in wife to James King of Cyprus, and when she was about to depart, many festivities took place in the City, and the Doge went to receive her on the Bucintaur at San Polo, and with Royal pomp accompanied her as far as the Lido, where she embarked on the Galleys that took her to Cyprus.

Venetian Chronicles Sacred and Profane, Printed in Venice by Francesco Tosi A.D. 1793.

family that numbers one doge among its members (their name, in the Venetian dialect, is 'Corner'). They were more interested in commerce than politics, and were very wealthy. Some much needed financial assistance to the future bridegroom prepared the way for Caterain's marriage to James of Lusignan. As his bride, she became Queen of Cyprus, Jerusalem and Armenia. These kingdoms, then held by the French family of Lusignan (originating in Poitou), were an offshoot of the crusades. Many rival claimants arose, as successive monarchs died or were dispossessed, for example Richard I (Coeur de Lion) and Henry III of England, and the princes of the House of Savoy. The titles continued to figure on parchment and illuminated scrolls, long after they had lost every connection with the places named.

Like governments in our own day, the rulers of the *Serenissima* were opposed to the export of valuta and did all they could to prevent it. They objected strongly to Venetian heiresses marrying foreigners. But in the case of Caterina Cornaro there was a political advantage to be gained: a virtual protectorate over the island of Cyprus. The Cypriotes did not want a Venetian protectorate, or foreign tutelage of any sort. But their geographical position—then as now—made of them a valuable piece on the chess-board of international politics. The poor girl was solemnly and officially adopted as the 'Daughter of the Republic'. Thus they kept a hold on her. Her departure became an occasion for that magnificent pageantry, for which Venice was justly famous.

Her reign was a brief one. Her husband died of a fever, one short year after their marriage, when she was with child. A boy was born in due course, but had small chances of succeeding to the throne, and died in infancy.

A rumour arose that Caterina might marry again and that her new husband might be the King of Naples—a rival of Venice in the Mediterranean. This was enough to alarm the Senate.

Every kind of pressure was brought to bear on the unfortunate

Caterina, to persuade her to abdicate in favour of the *Serenissima*—a step that she proved most unwilling to take. She liked her island kingdom. She was not averse to marrying Alfonso II of Naples. At first she flatly refused to give up her royal status. Kingship possessed in those days an acknowledged lure that our modern Press does its best to vulgarize and our materialistic philosophy to belittle—without wholly succeeding. An Island Queen, to reverence whom one had to sail—like the Argonauts—in the direction of the sunrise: is there not something here to fire the imagination? Something of the mystic charm that inspired Rostand's *Princesse Lointaine? On finit pour aimer tout ce vers quoi l'on rame!*

But Caterina was the adopted daughter of a strict parent, a parent who exacted unquestioning obedience. She was a patrician, and the first duty of a Venetian patrician—male or female—was to serve. *Noblesse oblige.*

She had to give in and return to Venice.

The bitter pill was sugared and gilded. Submission was made as pleasant as possible. She was allowed an income of 8,000 ducats, and given the small town and castle of Asolo, where she held a diminutive court which justified its existence by a classic culture and refinement. There Cardinal Bembo represented the *beau idéal* of the contemporary man of letters and spoke even Italian with a Ciceronian cadence. Asolo had always been popular with literary people. It is a charming backwater, and the swift-running stream of life passes it by. Caterina's feelings must have been similar to those expressed by Margaret of Parma in Goethe's play, *Egmont*: 'He who is used to command and had held in his hand the fate of thousands, steps down from the throne as into a grave. Better so than to live on as a ghost among the living.'[1]

Poor Caterina was a ghost long before she died. She has a

---

[1] '*Wer zu herrschen gewohnt ist, wer hergebracht hat, dass jeden Tag das Schickfal von Tausenden in seiner Hand liegt, steigt vom Throne wie in' Grab. Aber besser so, als einem Gespenste gleich unter den Lebenden bleiben. . . .*'

beautiful tomb in the church of San Salvatore. This is what Horatio Brown, in his *Venetian Studies*, says of her funeral:

> Caterina died in Venice on the 10th July 1510, fifty-six years old. On the eleventh a bridge of boats was made across the Grand Canal, from the Cornaro Palace to the other side. The dead Queen was followed by the Patriarch, the Signory, the vice-doge, the archbishop of Spalato, and an immense crowd of citizens with torches in their hands. There was something fitting in the manner of her burial, for the night was a stormy one, with heavy wind and rain. On her coffin lay the crown of Cyprus—outwardly at least, Venice insisted that her daughter was a Queen; but inside, the body lay shrouded in the habit of St. Francis, with a cord and cowl and coarse brown cloak. . . . On her grave Andrea Navagero, poet, scholar and ambassador, made an oration that bade farewell to this unhappy queen, whose beauty, goodness, gentleness, and grace were unavailing to save her from the tyrannous cruelty of fate.

*   *   *

Unlike Caterina Cornaro, Bianca Cappello was a thoroughly bad lot, and her fellow-citizens were ashamed of her (though possibly a little envious). She defied the Venetian Senate and got away with it.

Hers again was a rich and powerful family, but at the age of fifteen she ran away to Florence with Pietro Bonaventura, a small clerk in the firm of Salviati. He took her to the modest home of his father and mother, who expected Bianca to do some of the housework. But she refused.

Meanwhile the Venetian Senate was asking for her to be sent home to her family, to be treated as a naughty girl. But Bianca vamped the heir to the Grand Duchy, Francesco de Medici, an unprincipled rake, who covered her with jewels and installed her in a palace next to his own. Her husband raised no objection. *He* found plenty of consolation, ·apparently, with the ladies of the court.

Francesco was married to Giovanna, an Arch-Duchess of Austria, who bore him no children. When she died, Bianca hoped to produce an heir to the throne, as she had given birth to a daughter, Pellegrina, to her first husband. But no child came. . . .

The Venetian Senate, much to everybody's disgust, had to pay homage to Bianca as Grand Duchess of Tuscany. The rake's progress ended in an apotheosis. Desert and reward seldom keep company.

In 1585, Francesco and Bianca died within a few days of each other.

*   *   *

'The best part of beauty is that which a picture cannot express.' This is one of Francis Bacon's apothegms, and I'm not sure that I agree with him. But probably it is true of Marina Benzon (Countess Marina Querini Benzon). Longhi's formal portrait of her shows no vivacity in the sitter, and Marina was mercurial in character and in looks: quick, gay, scintillating like fluid metal that flashes back the light.

The most charming tribute that can be paid to a woman is to write a song about her, with an air that lingers in the hearts of her countrymen, after her beauty has faded and her place knows her no more. A song by Lamberti, called *La Biondina in gondoleta*, describes Marina—as Longhi's picture represents her —at a moment when she could not have been vivacious, but it conveys a charming picture of her.

> *La biondina in gondoleta*
> *l'altra sera go menà,*
> *dal piacer la povareta*
> *la s'a in bota indormenzà.*

meaning that the singer took the young fair girl out in a gondola and her enjoyment of the trip was such that the poor child immediately fell asleep!

Something in this fantasy seems to have stuck in the half-humorous, half-sentimental minds of Marina's countrymen: the sleeping girl in the boat that glides over the still water; the breeze fanning her cheek and stirring her garments, while her admirer watches over her tenderly:

The Marchesa Iris Origo wrote an article about Marina, in the autumn number of *Cornhill Magazine* for 1951. It begins:

When, in 1798, the troops of the French Directoire occupied Venice, a remarkable sight was to be seen in Piazza San Marco; a 'tree of liberty' was erected there, and round it, singing the 'Carmagnole', danced not only the Venetian populace, but some of the patricians who, infected by the general enthusiasm for the catchwords of equality and fraternity, had despoiled themselves of their titles, their jewels and their gala robes, and were proud to wear upon their head the 'bonnet de la liberté'. Among them, hand in hand with the handsome young revolutionary poet Ugo Foscolo, and dressed only in a short Athenian tunic which revealed her graceful legs and thighs, was one of the liveliest and gayest of the Venetian beauties: Contessa Marina Querini Benzon. But her enthusiasm for the French was of short duration. All too soon it became clear to the Venetians that the liberators had become despoilers. The contents of the Venetian granaries, arsenals, libraries and palaces were ransacked, the four horses of San Marco were borne off to the Louvre, the diamonds of the church's treasury were set in Josephine's crown. . . .

Here Marina is described when she was very young and—her figure being a good one—her charms were enhanced by a tunic such as girls once wore in Sparta. She and some of her peers in Venice were filled with the same generous enthusiasms that, in the first days of the Revolution, had inspired the French nobles to renounce their *droits seigneuriaux* at the *Serment du Jeu du Paume* (depicted in a picture by David).

Such enthusiasms seldom last long, especially when they imply—as they did in Venice—the presence of a foreign Army of Occupation.

When Byron came to Venice, he frequented her salon, and it was there that he met Teresa.

As a young widow, Marina had a faithful lover of her own, in Count Giuseppe Rangone of Padua (whom she ended by marrying), but she had a soft place in her heart also for Byron, who in his turn felt some affection for her and admired the warm spontaneous kindheartedness that pierced through the artificiality and gossip-mongering of a society in its decadence. He took no offence when she scolded him for his indiscreet behaviour with Teresa, possibly admitting that her reproaches might be justified. Certainly, they were kindly meant. Marina was nothing, if not kind.

He wrote to her from Greece, in 1824, not long before his death.

Marina was one of those people who have scant self-control. Very little over her emotions, and even less over her appetite. She became stout in early middle-age, being childishly greedy. She was nicknamed *il Fumeto*, because of a strange habit of taking slices of hot *polenta* (kept warm in her ample bosom) when starting out in a gondola to call on her friends, such as the Gradenigos, the Gonzagas, the Benetivoglios and Teresa Contarini. Passing gondoliers would see her munching the steaming *polenta* and laugh.

She was nearly always in debt, being unable to control her purse-strings or those of her son, Vittore, a poet in a small way, and a great admirer of Byron.

She died, at eighty-one, in 1863. The Venetians, who have forgotten so many more important people, still remember her: *la biondina in gondoleta.*

* * *

If, like the son of Priam, I had to choose between the comparative beauty of rival goddesses, it is only natural that I should favour the one I knew personally—not those whom I have merely read about!

Annina Morosini was perhaps the last of the great ladies to queen it in Venice, so much so that she was nicknamed 'la Dogaressa', as if we still lived in the days of the Doges.

Soon after she died, in 1954, an article appeared in a weekly paper, written by some woman who resented the chorus of admiration that exalted the really remarkable splendour of Annina's beauty. The writer said that her shoulders were heavy and her skin coarse in texture. What the disgruntled lady said about Annina's complexion was certainly untrue. That her neck and shoulders should no longer be swan-like was not surprising, as she was over eighty when she died. I saw her last in 1953, when she used to receive in a black velvet dress, very high in the collar. Her good looks, for a woman of that age, were still really astonishing.

I speak without bias, for her particular type of beauty was not that which attracted me most: the type of ample bosom and a waist well contained by stays. Hers was the beauty of the full-blown rose. I like the kind that holds the promise of greater things to come. But then, I only got to know her at all well when she was already middle-aged.

If I had first seen her when she was a young girl, I might have felt differently about it. It is also true that when she turned on me—sometimes in anger—the full blaze of her imperious eyes, I felt that I was indeed in the presence of a face that might have launched a thousand ships and burned the square-topped towers of Ilium.

Leone Caetani, who was one of her admirers (before he married the beautiful Vittoria Colonna) assured me that, as a girl, Annina had a very slim and willowy figure. He also told me a story which confutes the remarks of the acidulous lady-journalist who denied Annina's claims to a superlative physical attractiveness.

Annina's parents were not Venetian; they were the Rombos of Genoa. They happened to be travelling by train, with their young daughter, and they had a compartment to themselves.

Annina had stretched herself out on the seat opposite her parents and was fast asleep. Their train was due at its destination about midnight. It stopped at a wayside station and a young man got in. As Annina did not wake, he took a seat opposite her, next to her parents. And he gazed in evident stupefaction at the sleeping beauty before him. After half an hour of this contemplation, he got up and stepped into the corridor, making a sign to Rombo *père* that he wished to speak to him. When the elder man joined him, he took out a visiting card and said: 'This is my name. Is that your daughter, lying asleep?'

'Yes.'

'I want to marry her!'

It was a silly procedure, even though the owner of the visiting card turned out to be a wealthy man of good family (*Je suis un jeune homme pressé, mais modeste!*).

Nothing came of it.

There were stories and legends innumerable about Annina: some of them invented; some of them partially true, and others as near being true as such stories can be, which is not saying much. The subject was often her domineering character and the confident assumption that she was, in some way undefined, the ruling person in Venice. The government authorities pandered to her tyrannical spirit by asking her—as often as not—to receive in the Palazzo da Mula, where she lived, such royalties as might turn up to visit the town.

Annina was so sure of herself that it never occurred to her that the mere mention of her name was not sufficient to carry off any situation.

'I am the Countess Morosini,' was all the explanation she offered for going, unasked, on board the Drexel yacht, when it dropped anchor opposite the Punta della Salute. Those five words and a smile were indeed all that was required to bring her astonished hosts to her feet. Perhaps the smile would have been enough.

19

THE AMERICAN CONSUL

I could not have been more literary; but I have sometimes
wished I had been less ignorant.

WILLIAM DEAN HOWELLS—Preface to a reprint of his
Venetian Life

NOT when I wore an Eton jacket and trotted after Carlina
through the *calli,* but a few years later, when I was still a very
young man, I wrote a story in English, called *Milady.* I firmly
believe it was the very worst story that had ever been written
with Venice for its background. But at the time, I was rather
pleased with it. Indeed, I sent it, together with some other
stories, to the *Temple Bar* magazine, and I regret (now) to say
that it was printed.

I suppose it was not badly written, and plausible to the
uninitiated.

Only when somebody gave me *Venetian Life,* by William
Dean Howells, did I begin to realize what an appalling collection of impossibilities and mis-statements I had put together,
purporting to be the account of some events that had occurred
in Venice, in the years following the revolution of 1848.

These were the years when William Dean Howells was
American Consul. He knew the city in one of the saddest
periods of its history—the Venice that my father had known,
when he was sent into exile.

Among the consular duties was that of writing an annual
report, to be sent to Washington in September, about commercial relations. It was like making bricks without straw.

179

The material was wanting with which poor Howells could make a respectable show among his consular peers in ports like Marseilles, Liverpool and Bremen. Others could fill a much larger space in 'the handsomely misprinted' volume, issued every year by the Congressional publishers.

Howells complained that: 'It was with a feeling of profound mortification that I used to post my meagre account of a commerce that once was greater than that of all the rest of the world put together.'

Indeed the trade of Venice was then a ghost of the Rialto: a phantom of what it had been.

But meanwhile Howells was collecting, not commercial, but literary material and this was destined to come to life in his Memoirs, as a score of Beethoven breaks into music, under the baton of a master conductor.

There is no better *resumé* of the situation in the early 'sixties than the following:

Consigned to the Austrians by Napoleon I, . . . defeated in several attempts to throw off her yoke and loaded with heavier servitude after the fall of the short-lived Republic of 1849— Venice has always hated her masters with an exasperation deepened by each remove from the hope of independence, and she now detests them with a rancour which no concession short of absolute relinquishment of dominion would appease.

Instead, therefore, of finding that public gaiety and private hospitality for which the city was once famous, the stranger finds himself planted between two hostile camps, with merely the choice of sides open to him. Neutrality is solitude and friendship with neither party; society is the exclusive association with the Austrians or with the Italians. . . .

As for the carnival, which once lasted six months of the year, charming hither all the idlers of the world by its peculiar splendour and variety of pleasure, it does not any longer exist.

No lady of perfect standing among her people goes to the opera, and the men never go to the boxes, but if they frequent the theatre at all, they take places in the pit, in order that the house may wear as empty and dispirited a look as possible. Occasionally a bomb is exploded in the theatre, as a note of reminder, and as a means of keeping away such nobles as are not enemies of the government. In regard to the café, there is a perfectly understood system by which the Austrians go to one, and the Italians to the other.

It is in the Piazza that the tacit demonstration of hatred and discontent chiefly takes place. Here, thrice a week, in winter and summer, the military band plays the exquisite music for which the Austrians are famous. The selections are usually from Italian operas, and the attraction is of all others the hardest for the music-loving Italian to resist. But he does resist it. There are some ladies who have never entered the Piazza while the band was playing there, since the fall of the Republic in 1849.

The Austrians have a *casino*, and they give parties and balls, and now and then make some public manifestation of gaiety. But they detest Venice as a place of residence, being naturally averse to living in the midst of a people who shun them like a pestilence.

. . . It is impossible to believe that a people, which can maintain the stern and unyielding attitude now maintained by the Venetians toward an alien government disposed to make them any concession short of freedom, can be wanting in the great qualities which distinguish living peoples from those passed hopelessly into history and sentiment. In truth, glancing back over the whole career of the nation, I can discern in it nothing so admirable, so dignified, so steadfastly brave, as its present sacrifice of all that makes life easy and joyous, to the attainment of a good which shall make life noble.

The Venetians desire now, and first of all things, Liberty, knowing that in slavery men can learn no virtues. . . .

Every page, every paragraph, almost every line of *Milady*, by the present author, might have proved to W. D. Howells—supposing that he or his ghost had read the story—that this young Venetian with 'Risorgimento' antecedents, knew little or nothing about the subject of which he presumed to write. Well . . . every budding author, and sometimes even an old one, may occasionally make a fool of himself. And it all happened a long time ago. As we say in Italian, *è acqua passata che non macina più*. The water that has passed the mill-wheel will grind no more corn.

*   *   *

Howells was twenty-four when he first arrived in Venice, and began to write a diary: the diary of a literary man who is also simple and unworldly. Later he transcribed some passages from this diary, on very thin paper, in very bad handwriting, in the palest ink. He offered them for publication. Much to his disappointment, they were returned to him with a rejection slip. But a year or two later, he met the editor of the Boston *Advertiser*, passing through Venice, and this encouraged him to offer that journal a contribution about some contemporary event. It was printed. The former essays were printed too, and people liked them. Among those who showed their appreciation were James Lowell, first editor of the *Atlantic Monthly* (an office held by Howells himself between 1872 and 1881), and Motley, the American Minister in Vienna, who was the Consul's diplomatic chief.

Some of the pleasantest pages were about housekeeping in Venice. When I first read them, I was astonished at a foreigner having noticed so many things that I never had. This was because the things that appeared strange to him, I—from force of habit—took for granted.

He commented rather severely on the 'unsocial' domestic habits of Europe. Neighbours do not meet, except for some good reason. They merely bow as they pass on the common stairway, or in the street. To use Longfellow's simile, they are 'like ships that pass in the night, and speak one another in passing'. It astonished him that several families, living in one building, should see little or nothing of one another. Evidently he was not used to a house being divided up into separate apartments, each having a hall-door of its own, and each with a kitchen on a level with the other rooms of the dwelling to which it belongs.

In the details noted down by the Consul, I recognized some which might have been observed also in the apartment of my Aunt Caterina. For example, at the common entrance in the street below, was a line of metal bell-pulls, each with a name written above it and corresponding to one or other of the apartments above. You rang the bell under the name of the family on which you meant to call. A servant stuck her head out of some window above and asked: '*Chi x'è?*' ('Who is it?'). You answered '*Amici!*' ('Friends'). If the family was at home, the servant drew the latch of the outer door, by a wire running to her hand; if nobody was in, a basket was let down by a string from the window, to put a visiting-card in. And that was all.

The *piano nobile* was the best part of the building, but not necessarily the most comfortable. Howells was—or had to be—content with a smaller and cosier flat. Some of his windows looked down on a patch of garden, others upon the water of a canal, from which the morning sunlight was reflected on frescoed ceilings, dappling them with a tremulous, flickering light.

Gondoliers used to point out the house—Casa Falier—as that in which Marino Faliero was born. But this was only a myth, for the edification of strangers.

For a young man with a nature like that of Howells', the situation in Venice, during the last years of the Austrian domination, must have been personally very trying, as it was trying to everybody even to the Austrians themselves. The American Consul found it painful also because those were the years of civil war in the United States, and things were going badly at home.

Life became pleasanter when the Consul brought a young wife to Venice. A happy marriage offered a silver lining to the clouds of international politics. The newly wedded couple found a source of unfailing interest in the daily life of the lower classes, and fell—as many others, before and after them—into a state of resigned, delighted, or exasperated subjection to their domestic staff and other retainers, all of whom—as is the way with Italian servants—considered themselves as part of the family, especially after the arrival of a baby.

Living, at first, in close proximity to the Piazza and to St. Mark's, Howells soon fell under the spell of the Basilica. Its Byzantine magic and splendour appealed to his religious sentiment. He considered the dim interior as part of heaven.

But his family was of Quaker origin, and he had been brought up as a Swedenborgian. This made him instinctively antagonistic to the Roman Catholic Church. When Howells wrote his first books, there was a rather aggressive protestantism in the air. It is to be found in other authors, such as John Addington Symonds (especially in *The Catholic Revival*).

Given a bias against catholicism, it is natural that W. D. Howells' favourite character in Venetian history should have been the friar Paolo Sarpi, patriot, scholar and church reformer, who lived at a time when the Vatican was attempting to strain papal prerogative to the utmost, whereas Venice was adopting measures to restrict it over the entire territory of the Republic. It was Sarpi who fashioned the spiritual weapons, by which Venice resisted the bull of excommunication, launched against her by Pope Paul V (Borghese). This decree, had it been observed, would have deprived the Venetians of the consolations of their religion.

The quarrel arose over the determination of the Council of Ten to subject ecclesiastics, who were guilty of penal offences, to the secular laws. An Abbé and a Canon had been imprisoned, in defiance of the Pope's interference in their favour, nor did his threats obtain their release. Hence the excommunication of the City.

Priests should have closed their churches, refusing to say Mass. But one who attempted to do so, found a gibbet being erected in front of his house, and changed his mind. Another, who tried to run with the hare and hunt with the hounds, explained that, before deciding on a line of conduct, he must await the inspiration of the Holy Ghost. He was curtly informed that the Council of Ten had already received the inspiration of the Holy Ghost, authorizing them to hang any priest, who dared observe the papal Edict.

William Dean Howells felt a real sympathy for the Venetians who considered St. Mark, the apostle, as the equal of St. Peter, and their own Patriarch as the equal of the Pope.

In the religious conflict of A.D. 1606, the Venetians got the best of it, and were profoundly grateful to Sarpi, who had taken up their case as a theologian. Never before had a catholic ecclesiastic dared to maintain, in controversy with the Pope himself, the subjection of the clergy to the State.

Writing of this episode, W. D. Howells becomes lyrical in his admiration: 'Brave Sarpi and brave Republic! Men cannot honour them enough!'

He visited the Servite Convent where the friar had lived, and was disappointed to find it in ruins. The people he questioned were, one and all, ignorant of his hero. All that remained was a little tablet on the outside of a wall, speaking of the famous Theologue in an abbreviated Latin, difficult to understand. It said that Sarpi's ashes had been removed to the island of San Michele.

In the Preface (called 'The Author to the Reader') of a revised edition of his *Venetian Life*, Howells admits to have suppressed in it some Protestant transports concerning the simpler-hearted shows of Catholic piety, as he had first observed them: the votive offerings of arms and legs. . . . He had begun to see in these things the pathos of a humble faith, to which the more reasoned faith of the intellectualist should not refuse utterance.

The mellowed outlook of advancing years once inspired a story by Pirandello, called *La Fede* (Faith).

In this story, a young, spruce and highly intellectual priest, fresh from his theological studies in Rome, is sent to a remote village in the heel of Italy, to help the incumbent of a very poor parish, mostly populated by ignorant peasants. The priest whom this youthful cleric goes to serve, is old and ill and slovenly. His days are numbered. But he is loved by his parishioners, all of whom he knows personally, and likes and understands.

An old woman comes to the new arrival in the *parrocchia* and asks him to pray for her son, who is ill. She brings, as an offering, a chicken and three lire.

The young priest is full of zeal and good intentions; he will certainly say prayers for the son's recovery, as the poor mother wishes. But he needs no gifts to make him do so. It is his duty to God.

The old woman listens, but cannot understand. And because the priest will not take her offerings, her eyes fill with tears.

The junior cleric is puzzled, and goes to the older man, his chief, for advice. The ailing priest is very wheezy and asthmatic; he is lying on a rickety divan and has not shaved for days. He is not attractive to look at. He listens attentively to what his subordinate has to say, and answers:

Her faith is greater than yours. Take her three lire. Take her chicken. Pray for her son, and make her happy. Do not spoil with a small charity the far greater charity of that faith!

I think that W.D.H.—in his maturer years—would have understood and liked that story.

20

THE UNSUCCESSFUL GONDOLIER

The gondola is made for solitude or for company—the best
company, the company of two—as fancy may dispose. The
rower is out of sight behind. Nothing indicates movement
but the ripple and the lap of water under the bows, the
slow swaying of the steel *ferro* from side to side, and the
slower gliding by of palace fronts. There is no jolt of
springs, no rattle and bang of wheels, no noise of horses'
hoofs upon the road, above all, no dust; sea and sky are
in your sole possession, and the breeze just borne of the
gondola's progress; there is an infinite liberty of contemplation secured by space and solitude. . . . It is the boat for
leisure, not for business; the carriage of a leisured people;
all is quiet and deliberate. Life was not meant to be
bustled through and done with, by the men who
developed the gondola. . . .

HORATIO F. BROWN—*Life on the Lagoons*

'Tòdaro will never make a gondolier. He's too tall. He
ought to be a gladiator.'

'But, Mother, there aren't any gladiators left!'

'Quite true!' Mother spoke almost regretfully, as if the
disappearance of the *retarius* and the *secutor* were not a sign of
progress. 'But he's the image of the *Dying Gladiator* in the
Capitoline Museum. However, as he *is* in the army, he might
go into the King's Guard. He would look wonderful in a
burnished cuirass and an Achillean helmet.'

This conversation took place in Venice, between Mother
and myself, after we had been rowed down the Grand Canal

and round by Santa Chiara and the Giudecca, in a hired gondola, very inefficiently rowed by Tòdaro. (This was his Christian name. I don't remember his surname, supposing I ever heard it.) He came from Portogruaro and his parents and grandparents had been numbered among our family dependants in that small city. For this reason, Mother felt it encumbent on her to take a benevolent interest in his affairs.

It was the dream of Tòdaro's heart to be a gondolier. But, as we say in Italian '*era negato*'. That profession was denied him, on account of his great height.

Carpaccio's picture, *The Miracle of the Cross* (in the Accademia) gives a view of the old Rialto and the Palace of the Patriarch of Grado, as they existed at the close of the fifteenth century. It is the hour of sunset and the Grand Canal lies dusky at eventide, but the dark water throws into relief a crowd of gondolas, not black as they are now, but with canopies of gaily-coloured stuffs, and four light pillars. One of the gondoliers is a negro, very tall, and tricked out in almost fantastic finery; silken doublet, slashed sleeves, his dress enhancing the graceful gestures into which a gondolier naturally falls. The gondola is foreshortened, but even so, the height of the negro gondolier is no less out of proportion to his craft than Tòdaro's was, when rowing Mother and me on a trial trip, to show his prowess.

There are plenty of tall gondoliers, and they seem to manage all right. But Tòdaro's height was exceptional. He must have been six foot five. When he stood on the sloping piece of wood in the stern (the *punta piede*) and launched himself forward to the stroke, he often seemed in danger of falling over. Also, he could not pass under some of the bridges in the minor canals, without sitting down, or kneeling, and this, of course, was out of the question, when transporting people about the town.

Apart from the bridges, there are certain points where a gondola can hardly pass, even at low water: one near the Teatro La Fenice, and one near the Palazzo Mocenigo at San Stae. Also there are certain arches, underneath buildings, that

—for a gondola—are as difficult to thread as for a rich man to enter into the Kingdom of Heaven. There are two of these arches under Santo Stefano (you can see one of them from the bridge in the Calle dello Spezier). I have, occasionally, passed that way in a gondola, but only the most proficient of gondoliers attempt it, and only when the tide is out. For poor Tòdaro it was quite impossible.

So perfect is the gondola's structure that the poised oarsman, by a delicate turn of the wrist may take a boat where he will along the sinuous lines of that labyrinth of waterways. But it *does* require a special ability.

All the light craft of the lagoons are developed from the raft, flat-bottomed and capable of navigating shallow waters with a minimum of draught, and a maximum of load.

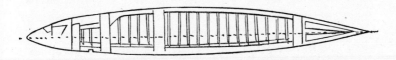

Luigi Zatta, champion of many regattas, once told me, with all the pride of an expert, that '*Per essere un buon gondoliere, bisogna venire da un ceppo di gondolieri*', meaning that a gondolier should come of a family of gondoliers, and prove himself a chip of the old block. Tòdaro came originally of mountain stock. His love of the sea, deep and sincere as it might be, was nevertheless an unfortunate one. '*Mi chiama il mare*' was an expression of his longing. Though the sea called him, he could not answer the call by plying an oar in the canals of Venice. In other days, he might have fought on a war-galleon at Lepanto.

The balance of a gondola is not like that of other boats. It is not built to lie perfectly flat on the water, but is tilted slightly to one side, and—on that side—sinks a little deeper. The axis is not in the centre and if a straight line is drawn from prow to poop, it will divide the gondola into unequal parts, the broader side being that where the rower stands. The high rowlock (made of walnut-wood and called *la forcola*) is on the narrower side. It follows that the rower has to exercise a very delicate control, in which he is helped by the accurate balancing of iron finishings for bow and stern, the *ferro da prora* and the *ferro da poppa*.

Like all boats, each gondola has a character and temperament of its own, and the gondolier's skill depends largely on his knowledge of his boat.

All this erudition—which I have acquired second-hand—may give the impression that I, myself, might have made a better gondolier than poor Tòdaro. But I doubt if this be true.

In G. A. Henty's book, *The Lion of St. Mark's* (a favourite of my early youth), the English boy, Francis, while living in Venice, is given a light gondola by his father, and learns to row it. When I was fifteen, I was fired by an ambition similar to Tòdaro's, and made several attempts to acquire a proficiency like that of Luigi Zatta. But I too was doomed to disappointment. While navigating the Canal della Giudecca, I collided with the small steam-boat that comes daily from Fusina. Fortunately, at the time, it was moving even slower than I was. Strange to say, in that incident the passengers on the steamer ran the greatest risk, for they all rushed simultaneously to the side whence they could observe a fool boy struggling in the water. By so doing, they might have provoked a serious accident.

After that episode I renounced all ambitions to become a gondolier. Mother was much disgusted with me. She said that, if I became discouraged at the first mishap, I would never become proficient in any sport or trade.

*   *   *

To go back to Tòdaro.

It was not only when negotiating sharp corners in narrow canals that the poor man got into difficulties, but also when rowing a gondola on the broad expanse of the lagoons, with nothing nearer than cloud-banks on the Friuli hills.

I suppose so much inefficiency might be put down to his ancestors, for he was not Venetian-born, nor did he belong to that indigenous race, which symbolized its ideals and its ambitions in the annual nuptials with the sea. I mean the ceremony that took place on the morning of the Ascension, when the Doge would stand on the stern of the Bucentaur and drop a golden ring into the water below. *Desponsamus te, mare.* . . .

Tòdaro appeared to be quite unconscious of the currents that ran under the seemingly quiet surface of the lagoon. Except in the immediate vicinity of the mainland, in the so-called 'dead-lagoon' (*laguna morta*), where the tides are hardly felt, those waters are never stagnant, never still. No danger of getting your oar tangled in the weedy stems of any aquatic plants.

Vivifying streams move continually in three separate submerged water-sheds between Torcello and the mouth of the 'Canale di Brenta', at Brondolo. What, at high-tide when the shoals are hidden, looks like one great lake, is intersected by a vast net-work of canals, through which flow the tidal waters that enter from the sea and return there, passing between the long, narrow islands that are the *lidi*. Even the bed of the lagoon is subject to continual changes and is disturbed by spring-tides and neap-tides, corresponding to the varying phases of the moon. Sometimes the Piazza itself is flooded, when high-tide is accompanied by the pressure of southern winds, blowing up the Adriatic. At other times (generally in February and March), some of the shallower canals run dry, and you may see a long black gondola, lying high and dry, like a stranded whale.

The more important waterways, in the lagoons themselves, are marked by pyramidal groups of posts, driven into the mud at regular intervals, to form an avenue. The separate posts are bound together near the top by metal bands, or cables. On some of these groups, there may be a tiny shrine to the Madonna, which passing boatmen decorate with flowers.

At night, one is guided by the alternating flashes of lighthouses on the outer islands, by the distant glow over Mestre, or by the lights of the city itself, burning on the water. But not Tòdaro!

He knew little or nothing of all this, and could only practise oarsmanship in his free hours. He was a *carabiniere*, enrolled in the military police, so it did not matter financially if he was not capable of following the calling of his dreams. In due course, as Mother had predicted (and I suspect she had a finger in the pie), he left Venice and came to Rome, to enter the King's Guard, as a *corazziere*. Their barracks stood exactly opposite the house in which Mother had taken an apartment, at 118 Via 20 Settembre.

When off duty, Tòdaro would often drop in to see us. In fact, he paid such frequent calls that Mother expressed the opinion that he might have a tender spot in his heart for Agnès. She was older than he was, and not exactly beautiful. When she passed along the Via 20 Settembre, the air was not thick with the soft words that follow a pretty girl down an Italian street. I don't think anyone ever called her *Carina*, or *Bellina*. But she was attractive in a robust, full-bosomed Teutonic way. She might have been compared to one of the nine daughters of Wotan, who used to descend from Valhalla, to carry up the warriors who had fallen in battle.

It may have been at Agnès's suggestion that Mother took Tòdaro down to Suscipi's in the Via Condotti, to be photographed. One copy was retained by Agnès and another pasted in a huge family album, with views of Scotland, of Venice, of the Dolomites and of the Italian Lakes.

The reason given for taking those photographs was the one which Mother had once mentioned to me: the marked resemblance between Tòdaro and the *Dying Gladiator* in the

Capitoline sculpture gallery. He is not a gladiator, really, but a Gaul. It is true that there was nothing Italian about Tòdaro's looks; nothing of the Latin race. He might have been one of the Gauls who, 250 years before the birth of Christ, invaded Asia Minor, and were repulsed by Attalus, King of Pergamum. To commemorate his victory, the King ordered some statues to be cast in bronze, statues representing those warriors who had fallen in battle, so far from home. Two copies, in marble, are to be seen in Rome; one in the Museum of the Thermae and one in the Capitol. The originals must have been numbered among the masterpieces of the so-called School of Pergamum.

The photograph taken of Tòdaro, at Mother's expense, shows him in uniform and wearing a cloak, and is intended only to present his head and the strangely alien-looking face. Though the expression is not that of the statue, drawn with pain and facing death, the resemblance is startling. I cannot help thinking that, if the portrait had been taken to-day (and not in the nineteenth century) Tòdaro would have been persuaded to pose in the attitude of the sculpture by Epigonos, and with no other clothing than the *torque* round his neck. But Mother had been born under Queen Victoria, and such realism was not to be thought of, as long as that monarch was on the throne.

*   *   *

I am aware that Tòdaro's ghost is not really entitled to haunt the Rialto. But I cannot help wishing that his heart's desire be realized in the world of shades and that he may row a phantom gondola, with the easy gliding motion of the *barcarolle* in the *Tales of Hoffmann*, up and down the Venetian canals. No need for the warning cries (*'Premi!—Stai!'*), by which living gondoliers herald their approach to a sharp corner.

And I can also imagine his tall figure, vaguely silhouetted against the pearly grey of the lagoons at dusk, and poised with a grace that he has now attained, in a gondolier's Valhalla, though he never possessed it in his lifetime. There is rhythm in his rowing, that follows the gentle swell on the water. The steel prow sweeps upwards, as if to reach the first evening star.

Is that Agnès, with him in the gondola? The light is fading, and it is difficult to see.

From a dark island near-by comes, very faintly, a tenor voice singing Lohengrin's good-bye to the swan:

Nun sei bedankt
Mein lieber Schwan!

But why Wagner? Why not *La biondina in gondoleta*?

21

THE CAMPANILE

Es war um Mittag und heller Sonnenschein, dass ich ohne Perspektiv Nähen und Fernen genau erkennen konnte. Die Flut bedekte die Lagunen, und als ich den Blick nach dem sogenannten Lido Wandte . . . sah ich zum ersten mahl das Meer und einige Segel darauf. . . .

GOETHE—*Italienische Reise*—30th September 1786

IF you are in Venice, on a warm summer night, lying in bed (supposing, of course, that you retired early enough), it may be that you will hear through the open window the sound of little lapping waves and, at midnight, the deep mellow note of one bell. This is La Mezza Terza, sometimes called La Pregadi, tolling in the belfry of the Campanile of St. Mark's. No other bell in the city may toll at midnight.

The Pregadi rings again at six o'clock in the morning, but at that hour her voice is lost in a mighty chorus of church bells, much disapproved of by some of the sleepy people it has awakened.

Historical associations crowd one upon the other. Among them, the fact that, from the Campanile, Goethe first saw the sea, and Galileo first saw the satellites of the planet Jupiter.

Galileo was not the original inventor of the telescope, but a mere rumour of the new invention reached him in Venice in June 1609, and that sufficed to set him on the track. On the 21st August, he climbed up to the top of the Campanile, in company with several patricians, among whom the next Doge,

Antonio Priuli. They scanned the horizon with a *preziosa macchinetta* that Galileo had brought with him.

The instruments that he created and perfected with his own hands were then directed to the study of the heavens. The satellites he was the first to observe were named by him the *Sidera Medicea,* after the Grand Duke of Tuscany, Cosimo II. The Venetian Senate had given Galileo a richly paid professorship for life. But he hoped for greater leisure in his native Florence. When he left the lagoons, he lost the protection of the *Serenissima* against the Sacred College in Rome, who saw in his teachings a threat to the settled beliefs of the time. He ended his days, poor and persecuted and blind, at Arcetri, in the hills above Florence. There he was visited by Milton, not yet blind himself.

On the 14th July 1902, the Venetians—and not the Venetians only—received a frightening shock, such as Londoners might feel, or the Viennese, if the clock tower of Westminster were to fall, or the Stephansdom. The Campanile of St. Mark's collapsed upon itself. Fortunately there was no loss of life, with the sad exception of the cat, who lived in the custodian's lodge below.

Rosolino Gattinoni spoke of this cat by the highly improbable name of 'Mélampyge', an animal who had been beloved, in its day, by Giacomo Casanova. I think this must have been a mere whim of Rosolino's, for Casanova's pet—the original bearer of the name—had been a dog, and not a cat. The English have several more or less popular expressions that correspond to 'monomania', or what in other languages is called *idée fixe, fixe idée,* or *fissazione.* An Englishman might have said of Rosolino, that, where the Campanile was concerned, he had 'a bee in his bonnet', or even more aptly, 'bats in the belfry'.

Apart from Venice itself, and everything that concerned his native city, Rosolino's monomania was the Campanile and the bells that the mighty steeple upheld. It was perhaps inevitable that it should be so, for on going in and out of the Marciana Library, he passed the base of the spire, and the so-called 'Loggia' of Sansovino, several times a day; and he could see it from the windows of the room in the upper story, where he worked.

It was he who told me that Mélampyge had been hurriedly picked up when her mistress—who was ironing some shirts at the time—was warned to leave the tower, which was in danger of falling. Pussy was taken into the Mercerie, where she might have been quite safe, but, with the instinct (or the cussedness) of her kind, on being released, she bolted back home and died —like a Roman sentinel—at her post.

If Rosolino once got on to the subject of the Campanile, he would let loose a perfect flood of erudition. And he would discourse learnedly on the past uses of bells, necessary even to the housewife in her kitchen, before the general use of clocks and watches in the home.

Bells brought good news to Zion, and they may still call soldiers to arms, as they do Christians to prayer. They ring in joyfulness, in sorrow and in anger. These are some of the things I learnt about them. The bells of the Campanile in Venice had different peals for different events. If you recognized them, you knew what was going on. There was a special peal to salute the merchant galleys returning from the East.

At Easter 1282, a Frenchman of the garrison held in Palermo by the house of Anjou insulted a girl who was on her way to church at Palermo, to hear Vespers with her bethrothed. The Sicilians, who were waiting for the opportunity to revolt, seized upon this incident to turn on their oppressors. The bells that rang for Vespers gave the signal and some 8,000 Frenchmen were massacred in cold blood. The 'Sicilian Vespers' have been known, since that day, as a symbol of revolt.

On the 21st August 1571, on the night of St. Bartholomew, the church bells in France ushered in the massacre of 100,000 Huguenots. In October 1805, the Church bells in England

rang out merry peals, alternating with one deep toll, to
hail the news of Nelson's triumph and death at Trafalgar.
So did the bells of the Campanile ring for the victory of
Lepanto.

Naturally, it was from Rosolino that I heard the history of
our Campanile, and the reasons for its collapse.

The structure's great age, the added weight of additions
made as far back as the year 1510, some imprudent cutting
away inside the lower part of the tower (as if it were not subject
to the mechanical rules of statics), all contributed to the
catastrophe. The foundations, old as they were, still held good.
When reconstruction began, they were found to be in excellent
condition. Giacomo Boni, the archæologist who excavated the
Roman Forum, had examined the foundations of the Venetian
Campanile, as far back as the year 1885. He discovered seven
strata of stone, followed by what he called a 'zatterone'
(a kind of raft) of wood, and finally piles as in a prehistoric lake
dwelling. What astonished Boni (perhaps more than discovery
of the *lapis niger* in the Forum) was to find that the foundations
of the Campanile, which was 320 feet high, did not descend
more than about 28 feet, whereas a local legend described them
as penetrating far lower, under the surface paving of the
Piazza and then spreading out on every side in the shape of a
star.

After the catastrophe of July 1902, the old foundations
were examined again, and it was confirmed that they were in
no way responsible for the fall of the structure they had so
bravely upheld, for so long. The original piles on which the
Campanile had been laid had not rotted away; they had become
fossilized and were as firm as ever.

Not everyone was sorry when the old Campanile fell. My
cousin Nane, entering the Piazza soon after the catastrophe,
exclaimed delightedly: '*Meno male!*' (a local equivalent for
'Thank Heaven!'). Nane thought that the Piazza looked better
without the isolated tower in one corner, and that, if we must

have a Campanile, it should be set up elsewhere. (Unlike the steeples of northern churches, the southern *campanili* are not usually attached to the church.)

Not a few people agreed with Nane. When the question arose whether the Campanile should be rebuilt and where, many were the divergent views expressed in the newspapers and in Parliament. In the end—thanks principally to Pompeo Molmenti—it was decided that it should rise again where it had been and as it had been.

The new Campanile is a faithful replica of the old, and built, in part, with the old material.

The first piles of the old tower had been driven into the mud, as foundations of the Campanile, on the 25th April of the year 912.

The new Campanile was inaugurated 1,000 years later: 25th April 1912. It had taken ten years to build.

Of the five bells, four had been broken in the fall. One only remained intact: the biggest, the Marangona. It lay pillowed and unhurt on the rubble.

The four other bells were re-founded and hung up at the expense of Pope Pius X, who thus gave one more proof of his affection for Venice.

And Rosolino Gattinoni wrote a book about it all, called *Storia del Campanile di San Marco in Venezia.*

When the last of the débris was taken away, and the work of rebuilding was about to begin, six shirts were found in the custodian's lodge. The custodian's wife had been ironing them when she had been told to make her escape, before the spire fell. The shirts were as good as new. They only required to be washed and ironed once more. They belonged, I was told, to Jesurum, owner of the lace-making firm.

In July 1912, at the official banquet given to celebrate the rebirth of the Campanile, six of the assembled guests wore a shirt that had been buried under the débris. I believe it was a lasting sorrow to Rosolino that he was not numbered among the important personages, entitled to wear one of Jesurum's shirts at the banquet!

But his book is there to associate him with his beloved Campanile; and all the history of Venice, except the earliest beginnings, is there, in the story of the Campanile, the City's watchtower. It is the tale of a civilization that, from the humblest beginnings, rose to a zenith of grandeur and of power and declined in a mellow twilight.

Rosolino's book starts with Pietro Tribuno, the Doge who laid the foundations, and Pietro Partecipazio, who began to build the walls. He tells of the fire that destroyed the Doge's palace and injured the surrounding buildings, during the revolt against the Candianis, who attempted to set up an absolute monarchy. After them, the saintly Pietro Orsenigo (subsequently canonized) spent enormous sums of his own in rebuilding the Basilica and raising the Campanile to a height a little above that of the surrounding houses. There were long interruptions in the tower's growth; the longest being thirty-five years. Old Venetian names recur in those of the doges who, from time to time, ordered the work to be resumed, or allowed it to be suspended.

When it was finally completed, the Venetian mania for gilding became a source of trouble. The pointed spire, raised to surmount the belfry, was made of richly gilded brass. The gold-coated surface could be seen by ships far out at sea, flashing in the sunlight, much as a lighthouse flashes at night. But that huge metal point drew the lightning, time after time. Finally a safer spire was set up, made of wood, with an outer surface of coloured stone.

It is a common idea, in Italy, that the mediæval towers speak to one another, across the plains and the mountain valleys, as over the roofs of a town. Thus Carducci imagines a dialogue between the two square leaning towers in Bologna, known as Asinella and Garisenda. They recall the barbarian invasions; the clash of Guelph and Gibelline swords in the streets at their feet; the meeting between Emperor and Pope, to curb Italian liberties.

Nothing strange, then, that the old Campanile, as its last hour was approaching should have called to its brothers, the bell-towers on the islands and on the mainland, as far as the Alps and the Euganean Hills: 'Stand fast, for I fall! Farewell, farewell, farewell!'

That day, for the first time in ten centuries, the bells of the Campanile did not ring. The other towers waited in vain for the Marangona to give them the midday signal to raise their voices over land and sea. They rang out, and even as they did so, the oldest tower of them all subsided with a last sob of despair. And a great cloud of dust mounted up into the sky, hiding the ruin, as if with a shroud.

22

THE LITTLEST GHOST OF ALL

It was a fortnight after Allegra's death, and only two months before he himself set sail on this same sea, that Shelley, whilst walking with Williams on the terrace of Casa Magni, thought he saw the figure of a child rising out of the waves. It disappeared. Then, clutching his friend's arm, 'There it is again, there!' he cried. Allegra was coming towards him in the moonlight, clapping her hands as if in joy, and smiling at him.

IRIS ORIGO—*Allegra* (last paragraph)

'WHOM the gods love die young.'

This old saying is Menander's. It reappears in Byron's *Don Juan* and the idea comes again in *Childe Harold*. Perhaps it applies to his own illegitimate daughter, who died at Bagnocavallo, near Ravenna, she being then only five years old and three months.

Descriptions of her agree that she was a beautiful child. Clever she certainly was, learning to read and write before children older than herself. When very small, she had been fair, but at three years old her hair began to darken. Her eyes were blue and possibly she might have inherited her father's 'fatal pallor'.

Writing to his sister, soon after the child's birth, Byron said: '. . . I must love something in my old age, and probably circumstances will render this poor little creature a great, and, perhaps, my only comfort.'

The mother was Jane Clairmont, who liked to be called

'Claire'. Iris Origo describes her as '. . . an impulsive, emotional, capricious young woman, with dark hair, dark eyes, olive cheeks, a quick but untrained intelligence, an unstable exacting nature, and an intense eagerness for any romance and adventure.'

Claire wished that Allegra should have an education 'becoming to the child of an English nobleman', and against all advice agreed that she should be entrusted to her father's care, though this involved separation from herself. It was therefore with its mother's consent that Byron had the child sent to him in Venice, where he was living in the Palazzo Nani-Mocenigo,[1] on the Grand Canal. In former times, this palace had been occupied by the Duke Emanuel of Savoy, who came there after the battles of Mühlberg and Saint Quentin; also by Giordano Bruno, who afterwards went to Rome, where he was burnt at the stake by the Inquisition.

When taken to Venice, little Allegra passed from the quiet home life, shared with the children of Percy and Mary Shelley, to the agitated, unconventional existence of Bohemia (though it may be difficult to think of the Palazzo Nani-Mocenigo as Bohemia, even when occupied by Byron).

In the hierarchy of poets, Percy Bysshe Shelley stands higher than Byron. William Rossetti wrote of him: 'If we except Goethe, we must consider Shelley to be the supreme poet of the new era which, beginning with the French Revolution remains continuous into our own day. Victor Hugo comes nearest to him in poetic stature . . .; Byron and Wordsworth also have their numerous champions—not to speak of Tennyson and Browning.'

Shelley was a lover of babies: of his own babies and of

---

[1] Foreigners are often puzzled to locate the Palazzi where notabilities in Venice have resided. This comes from the fact that many different Palazzi bear the same name. There are no less than eleven houses called Palazzo Giustinian. There are three houses called Palazzo Mocenigo on the Grand Canal going from the Rialto towards St. Mark's. The one Lord Byron lived in was the third, sometimes called 'Palazzo Mocenigo vecchio'.

Allegra. He was destined to suffer acutely as, one after another, they all died in childhood.

Allegra and her mother had lived in the house of Percy and Mary Shelley at Great Marlow. She went with them to Italy, to the Villa Pliniana on Lake Como, and from there passed into her father's care. Her short life was one of many changes, like a tender plant that gets potted and re-potted in different soils and climates.

As was to be expected, the poet-peer's ménage was not a suitable one for a child. Large, gloomy halls with high frescoed ceilings. Cold marble floors. Caged animals (among them, a wolf), besides dogs and monkeys, wandering round unhappily. A noisy, violent, passionate woman, Margherita Cogni, attempted to rule the household in her quality of milord's temporary mistress. She was the baker's wife, and therefore spoken of as 'la Fornarina'. Allegra may not have been consciously unhappy, but she was alternately spoilt and neglected. She must have missed her mother, her little playfellows, Shelley's gentle kindness and understanding, and the homely atmosphere of an unpretentious country-house.

What are gold and myrrh and frankincense, such as the three kings brought to Bethlehem; what are the gilding, the marble, the pictures and sculptures of a palace rising from the sea, compared to the cosy primness and the hours of play and make-believe in an old nursery?

After her arrival at her father's house, Allegra was rarely allowed to see her mother, who was also in Italy, staying most of the time with the Shelleys. Later, she became a governess to an Italian family in Florence, probably a very bad governess, for she was a silly woman. Byron was—to say the least—an injudicious parent; so was Claire.

Most of the members of that group of talented, undisciplined people were destined for tragedy. Little Allegra was the victim of her parents' passion and antagonism.

If Claire had been seduced by Byron, his subsequent conduct

towards her would have been unpardonable. But it was she who had forced herself upon him, her unbalanced mind being imbued with theories of freedom in love (as an attenuating circumstance, one should keep in mind that she may have got these ideas from Shelley). At first, Byron had not responded to her advances, taking no notice of the letters he received from this unknown female. Probably it was the discovery that she was connected with the Shelleys which first aroused his interest. Claire was the step-daughter of William Godwin, whose own daughter, Mary, had eloped with Shelley (if elopement is the right expression for going off with a man, who was already married to someone else). There was no blood relation between Claire and Mary, but she attached herself to the amorous couple like a barnacle to a ship's keel, and at times must have tried their patience extremely.

Byron and Claire had met and separated in the spring of 1816. Allegra was born in January 1817.

On various occasions, Byron expressed the wish that the child should be brought up as a Roman Catholic and that, when she grew up, she should make a respectable marriage, but with a foreigner, not a British subject. With this end in view, he settled five thousand pounds on her, as a *dot*.

Having such plans for the child's future, it was perhaps not unreasonable to make sure that Allegra should not be subject to her mother's influence. And Claire had the knack of exasperating Byron. Her pleading letters to him were often miracles of tactlessness and prejudice. He soon became callous and showed himself almost vindictive. Shelley would endeavour to mediate, in the child's interest, but nearly always in vain.

For one brief period, when living in Venice, Byron did allow little Allegra to stay with Claire and the Shelleys, in a villa he had rented for the purpose in the Euganean Hills. Allegra may have been contented there, but the sojourn cannot have been a happy one for the others. Mary Shelley was mourning for the recent death of her own little girl, and Claire watched the days slipping by in which her child would be with her.

After Venice, Allegra was taken by her father to Ravenna, where Teresa Guiccioli befriended her and did the best for her that the rather peculiar circumstances would allow. She took the child out driving in her carriage and showed her some of the gaieties of the carnival.

In Venice, the British Consul, Hoppner, had pointed out to Byron how unsuitable it was that a small child should live with him in the Nani-Mocenigo palace, and he and his wife had taken Allegra, for a time, to stay with them. Byron's existence in Ravenna began to be complicated by political activities and his sympathies with Italian revolutionists. Again, the unsuitableness of having a small child in his household became only too apparent. On one occasion, Allegra heard the groans of a wounded man being taken into the house to die. It was doubtless Teresa Guiccioli who advised her lover to place the child in charge of the Capuchin nuns at Bagnocavallo, a move which provoked passionate and unwise protests from Claire. Her natural possessiveness was expressed in letters which appear utterly unreasonable.

In various publications concerning Allegra, it is said that the child was first taken to Bagnocavallo by one Pellegrino Ghigi, an employee of the Guicciolis. How this small mistake arose I could not say. Pellegrino Ghigi was nobody's employee, but a gentleman of Ravenna, who directed a 'family bank' of his own, and put himself at the disposal of the English *milord* out of friendliness and courtesy towards a foreigner.

There were, and still are, various convents at Bagnocavallo. The one which Allegra was sent to had only recently returned to be administered by a religious order, after having been suppressed, during the Napoleonic wars, at the time when French troops first entered Romagna. The building was then bought by Count Paolo Gaiani, who later sold it again to Suora Marianna, the Mother Superior of the Capuchin nuns, who were organizing a school (an *educandato*) for girls between the ages of seven and sixteen.

Allegra, at four years old, had not attained the age for admittance. But on payment of double fees, and on the understanding that she should be under the personal care of the Mother Superior herself, the child was accepted and, from all accounts, was happy there and well cared for.

On arrival, she held out her hand for the nuns to kiss and insisted that she should take precedence of her companions in everything. Alternating neglect and over-indulgence had made of her a very spoilt little girl. The new atmosphere of modesty, order, regularity and kindness was, for her, most salutary.

Had it not been for certain not infrequent epidemics of fever, that broke out in the neighbourhood and were accepted as natural and unavoidable events in the community, the convent-education might have ended happily.

On 6th June 1821, Claire dreamt that she had received a letter to say that Allegra was ill and not likely to live. At first she does not seem to have been much alarmed. The joy of wakening and finding it was a dream and nothing more, seems to have prevented her from taking it as a premonition. But gradually her anxiety and the desire to get the child out of the convent became almost hysterical. She tormented herself and the Shelleys even more than before.

*   *   *

I was surprised to read, on 21st June 1955, in the afternoon edition of the *Corriere della Sera*, the account of a pilgrimage made by an Italian journalist, Francesco Serantini, to Bagnocavallo, to visit the place and the convent, where Allegra lived, and where she died of typhoid in April 1822.

Serantini does not quote books, but gives his own impressions of Bagnocavallo and of the convent, as it is to-day. Since 1842, he says, the convent does not take girls in as *educande*.

The nuns live—thirty of them—in *clausura*, in absolute retirement, in prayer and charity. They rise at dawn, and at midnight repair to chapel for an hour. They speak to visitors unseen, from behind a *ruota* (a wheel that can be used for passing parcels or letters). They read no newspapers.

The swamps of Comacchio (now being explored for buried cities) are close at hand, but the air is salubrious. Possibly it was less so in Allegra's time. Certainly in her day the nuns were not up-to-date, even for those times, with regard to precautions against contagion and matters of hygiene.

The general impression given by the countryside is that of the Georgics: '*Heu, fortunatos nimium, sua si bona norint, agricolas. . . !*' Bagnacavallo lies in the most fertile plain in Europe: the lower valley of the Po. Before the grain is harvested, the villages, the farms and the inhabitants seem to sink into a golden haze of ripening corn. Quiet rivers flow lazily to the sea, between huge dykes. In the distance, a chain of mountains (the Etruscan Apennines) ends eastward with the dim outline of a precipitous rock, Monte Titano, on which perches the little Republic of San Marino. This peaceful land was once dominated by a brigand called Passatore, and it is believed that a treasure, accumulated by him, lies hidden somewhere among the rich farms that doze in the heat of long summer afternoons.

It may be that Byron has been censored too severely in the matter of his treatment of Allegra and of Claire. If the child had lived, no one would now remember that he took no notice of her little letters, in Italian, asking him to come and see her. Or of his broken promise, made to Shelley, to go to Bagnacavallo. Byron was never a loving parent and his neglect of Allegra shocked Pelligrino Ghigi, who expressed regret that he had ever known him.

After Allegra's death, Byron was—or professed to be—in despair, admitting that he had troubled little about her when she was alive, but saying that he could not do without her, when she was dead. This did not prevent him protesting against the high cost of funeral expenses and of embalming.

He had the body transported to England, to Harrow, wishing it to be buried in the church there, with an inscription written by himself, which ran:

In Memory of
ALLEGRA
Daughter of G. G. Lord Byron
who died at Bagnacavallo
in Italy, April 20th 1822
Aged five years and three months . . .
'I shall go to her, but she shall not return to me'

2 SAMUEL XII. 23

In this quotation, the gender is changed. David was speaking of the child, a boy, born to him by the wife of Uriah the Hittite.

The Churchwarden at Harrow refused to allow Allegra's body to be buried inside the church. She lies in the churchyard, and no inscription marks her resting place.

There is a letter of Shelley's often quoted, describing little Allegra as she was, when he went to see her in the convent-school. She was dressed in a muslin frock and pantalets. She was shy at first, but brimmed over with pleasure when her visitor gave her the presents he had brought: a little gold cross and chain, and some candied fruits (which she ran off to share with her school friends). She was vain of her prowess with a skipping-rope and enjoyed showing off her room, with its little bed, and her numerous dolls. These dolls were so big that, after Allegra's death, the carpenter's wife, Marianna Foschini, used some of their garments to dress her own small children.

The last toy Allegra played with was a little figure of the Madonna, some eighteen inches high, in grey satin, with waxen head and hands and a gilt metal crown. Not the sort of doll a child might cuddle up to in bed! After Allegra's death, the nuns gave this toy to her special school-friend, Elettra Malagola.

It now belongs to the Marchesa Iris Origo, who showed it to me, when my wife and I went to see her at La Foce, in the province of Siena, one day in the autumn of 1955.

Soon after Allegra first entered the convent as an *educanda*, Byron sent his little daughter a gorgeous robe that he had worn in Parliament, as a Peer of the Realm. The idea was that it should be cut up to make a frock for Allegra. This, naturally, was never done. Either the nuns used it to make a curtain, or the priest took it! There are different versions of the *robone's* final destination.

Allegra herself had similar grandiose and impractical ideas about her wardrobe. When Shelley—on the day he visited her—asked what message he should take to her mother, she answered:

'Tell her to send me a kiss and a pretty frock!'

'What is the frock to be made of?'

'All of silk and gold!'

Poor Allegra! Hers is so very short a story, and hers must be such a very little ghost. Let us imagine her, not as Shelley thought he saw her after her death—a vague white form among the white crests of the waves—but like a little Infanta of Spain, painted by Velasquez, in a magnificence worthy of Venice! This is how she would like us to remember her.

IN MEMORIAM

While this book was in the hands of the printers, Daniele Varè died suddenly in Rome. The Laughing Diplomat has joined the shades which he has described so vividly, nostalgically, almost affectionately, in *Ghosts of the Spanish Steps* and now, in his last book, *Ghosts of the Rialto*. After a life of travel and interests in many lands he still lives on in his books, admired and remembered by countless friends and readers.

INDEX OF NAMES